ULTIMATE COSPLAY ENCYCLOPEDIA
VOLUME 1

/ARMOR UP!/
COSPLAY PROPS, ARMOR & ACCESSORIES

Thermoplastics

CHRISTOPHER TOCK *of* TOCK CUSTOM

CHAD VAN WYE *and* **SAMMY VAN WYE** *of* HOKU PROPS

FanPoweredPRESS
IMAGINE | MAKE | BECOME

PUBLISHER: Amy Barrett-Daffin

CREATIVE DIRECTOR: Gailen Runge

SENIOR EDITOR: Roxane Cerda

EDITOR: Liz Aneloski

COVER/BOOK DESIGNER: April Mostek

PRODUCTION COORDINATOR: Tim Manibusan

PHOTOGRAPHY COORDINATOR: Lauren Herberg

PHOTOGRAPHY as noted on photos or at right.

FRONT COVER ARTWORK by Christopher Tock

Published by C&T Publishing, Inc., P.O. Box 1456, Lafayette, CA 94549

Published by FanPowered Press, an imprint of C&T Publishing, Inc., P.O. Box 1456, Lafayette, CA 94549

Library of Congress Cataloging-in-Publication Data

Names: Tock, Christopher, 1984- author. | Van Wye, Chad, 1987- author. | Van Wye, Sammy, 1990- author.
Title: Armor up! : thermoplastics & modern materials : cosplay props, armor & accessories / Christopher Tock of Tock Custom, Chad Van Wye and Sammy Van Wye of Hoku Props.
Other titles: Thermoplastics & modern materials
Description: Lafayette, CA : FanPowered Press, an imprint of C&T Publishing, Inc., [2023] | Series: Ultimate cosplay encyclopedia ; volume 1 | Summary: "Included inside is everything beginner and expert cosplayers need to know for safely and successfully working with various plastics and synthetic materials. Cosplayers will also have access to a large collection of techniques on how to modify, color, heat form, and detail with these materials"-- Provided by publisher.
Identifiers: LCCN 2022031330 | ISBN 9781644032350 (trade paperback) | ISBN 9781644032367 (ebook)
Subjects: LCSH: Costume design. | Cosplay--Equipment and supplies. | Handicraft. | Armor. | Character actors and actresses.
Classification: LCC TT633 .T66 2023 | DDC 746.9/2--dc23/eng/20220822
LC record available at https://lccn.loc.gov/2022031330

Printed in China

10 9 8 7 6 5 4 3 2 1

INSTRUCTIONAL/ADDITIONAL PHOTOGRAPHY PROVIDED BY:

Multiple pages/cover (Swirl texture): Shutterstock.com/Karina Sofit

Page 9 (top right): Tock Custom

Page 9 (middle) and page 10: Tiffany Gordon Cosplay

Pages 12–15: Tiffany Gordon Cosplay

Pages 18–20: Sayakat Cosplay

Pages 21–26: Tiffany Gordon Cosplay

Pages 29–37: Sameer Tikka Masala

Pages 39–42: Panterona Cosplay

Pages 43–46: Tiffany Gordon Cosplay

Page 47: Tock Custom

Pages 50–60: Tock Custom

Pages 62–71: Alkali

Page 72, 75–77: Paisley and Glue

Page 78: Tock Custom

Page 79 (top left) and page 80 (top left): Maggie Hofmann

Pages 81–86: Paisley and Glue

Page 87: Chad Van Wye

Pages 88–94: Tiffany Gordon Cosplay

Pages 97–100: Mulholland Art

Page 101: Tock Custom

Pages 102–103: Tiffany Gordon Cosplay

Page 104: Candace Birger

Pages 107–112: Plexi Cosplay

Page 115: Chad Van Wye

Pages 117–121: Frostbite Cosplay

Pages 123–128: Polygon Forge

Page 130: Chad Van Wye

Pages 131–137: Polygon Forge

Page 139: Chad Van Wye

Pages 140–141: Frostbite Cosplay

Pages 144–151: Hoku Props

Page 152: Dave Kramer—Prop Monkey Studio

Pages 153–165: Dave Kramer—Prop Monkey Studio

Page 168 (top left): Ultimate Cosplay

Page 168 (top right): Hoku Props

Page 168 (bottom): Frostbite Cosplay

Page 169: Brett Downen—Downen Photography

Pages 170–171: Tock Custom

Page 174 (top right): Hoku Props

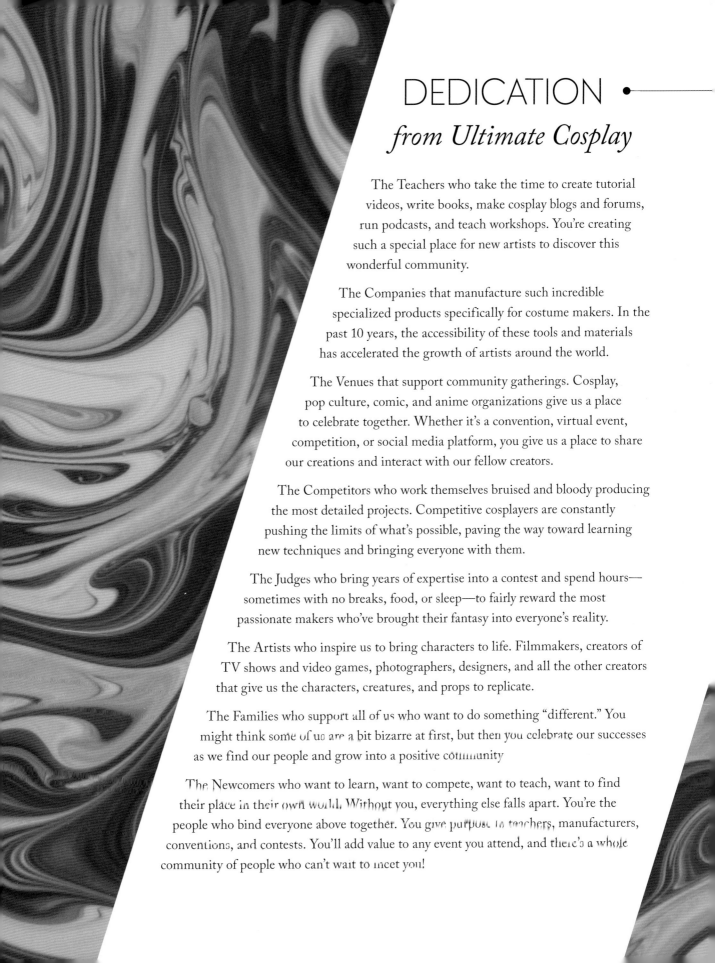

DEDICATION

from Ultimate Cosplay

The Teachers who take the time to create tutorial videos, write books, make cosplay blogs and forums, run podcasts, and teach workshops. You're creating such a special place for new artists to discover this wonderful community.

The Companies that manufacture such incredible specialized products specifically for costume makers. In the past 10 years, the accessibility of these tools and materials has accelerated the growth of artists around the world.

The Venues that support community gatherings. Cosplay, pop culture, comic, and anime organizations give us a place to celebrate together. Whether it's a convention, virtual event, competition, or social media platform, you give us a place to share our creations and interact with our fellow creators.

The Competitors who work themselves bruised and bloody producing the most detailed projects. Competitive cosplayers are constantly pushing the limits of what's possible, paving the way toward learning new techniques and bringing everyone with them.

The Judges who bring years of expertise into a contest and spend hours—sometimes with no breaks, food, or sleep—to fairly reward the most passionate makers who've brought their fantasy into everyone's reality.

The Artists who inspire us to bring characters to life. Filmmakers, creators of TV shows and video games, photographers, designers, and all the other creators that give us the characters, creatures, and props to replicate.

The Families who support all of us who want to do something "different." You might think some of us are a bit bizarre at first, but then you celebrate our successes as we find our people and grow into a positive community

The Newcomers who want to learn, want to compete, want to teach, want to find their place in their own world. Without you, everything else falls apart. You're the people who bind everyone above together. You give purpose to teachers, manufacturers, conventions, and contests. You'll add value to any event you attend, and there's a whole community of people who can't wait to meet you!

Dedication from Chris Tock

To my FAMILY (Dad, Mom, Kelly, Richard, Nate, Mike, Dave & Auntie Beth) for helping me focus on my physical, mental, spiritual, and emotional health throughout my life, my recovery, and my creative career. I never would have been able to pursue these goals without your help; turbo love forever!

It would not have been possible to achieve anything without the support and direction of all the amazing artists along the way. I have infinite gratitude to Evil Ted, Punished Props, Hoku Props, Kamui Cosplay, Volpin Props, Yaya Han, Coregeek Creations, my Twitch Creative & YouTube community, and all my maker friends.

Dedication from Chad

To my mom, April. Words could never express how much you mean to me, but an adoring son's gotta try when the occasion arises. Thank you for teaching me to do the right thing, even when no one is watching. For always telling me what I needed to hear instead of what I wanted to hear. For having the patience of a saint when I am not at my best. For showing me what true unconditional love is. For being my home. Your strength, grace, and support have made me the man I am today. I wish I could thank you from the bottom of my heart, but for you, my heart is bottomless. I love you.

And to the rest of my family, without everyone's love and support, none of this would have been possible.

P.S. Sorry for blowing up my face, LOL.

Dedication from Sammy

To my best friend and sister I never had, Kelly. Meeting you is the reason I believe in fate. Because let's be real, the likelihood of two twelve-year-old otaku girls from SoCal finding each other on a message board dedicated to making themes for AOL Instant Messenger and our parents agreeing to chaperone our first in-person meeting is absolutely insane sounding. Thank you for being my first real friend when all I knew were bullies and for cosplaying with me for all these years. Without you, I never would have had the courage to make my Noel dress "shorter."

And to my mothers, Lauren and Pauline. We all know I was terrible at basketball, so thank you for buying me a sewing machine to support my nerdy hobby instead. I love you both so much.

Acknowledgments

We are truly grateful for the artists who have come together to make this volume possible.

ALKALI

FROSTBITE COSPLAY

HOKU PROPS

MULHOLLAND ART

PAISLEY AND GLUE

PANTERONA COSPLAY

PLEXI COSPLAY

POLYGON FORGE

PROP MONKEY STUDIO

SAYAKAT COSPLAY

TIFFANY GORDON COSPLAY

TOCK CUSTOM

Special thanks to C&T Publishing for working with our team to produce such a high-quality technical manual. We understand that cosplayers can certainly be overambitious and disorganized, so you really deserve a lot of credit for putting up with us!

CONTENTS

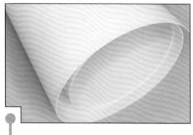

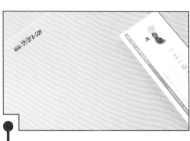

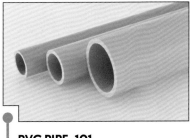

Introduction

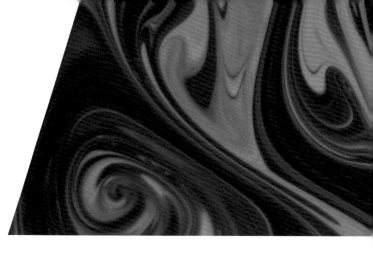

Cosplay as a performative art has come a long way from its humble beginnings on convention floors and small fan-run gatherings. Within the past ten years, it has become an international sensation that is practically a household name today. It's easier than ever to find information about how to cosplay, but as the popularity of cosplay continues to grow, so do the materials.

With the abundance of options and materials available now, it can be overwhelming to find a comfortable place to start for both beginners and cosplay veterans looking to expand their skill sets. Ultimate Cosplay and its global community wanted to find a way to help those who were struggling by creating a series of books that explore all the ins and outs of cosplay.

This first volume features an introduction to modern plastics commonly used in the cosplay and prop-making communities to make costumes, armor, and props. Within you will find many demonstrations from artists around the world, along with their personal insights on how to work with these materials.

The goal of this book is to provide a wide variety of fabrication techniques as well as personalized tips and tricks for each specific material. This book is a primer for expanding an artist's skills, but the techniques displayed in these demonstrations are not the be-all and end-all. We encourage you to continue to experiment, modify, and find new methods that work best for you, in hopes that one day you can spread that knowledge to the cosplay community too.

Worbla

What Is Worbla?

When most people hear the word *thermoplastics* in cosplay, they typically think of Worbla. With a variety of products, Worbla's applications can help everyone from beginners to experts achieve incredible results.

Uses

Worbla is easy to sculpt, and 100% of its scraps can be used to mold an object or add details to a piece. Worbla can be used to cover items such as cardboard, EVA foam, and insulation foam, or it can be molded over an object and used as is.

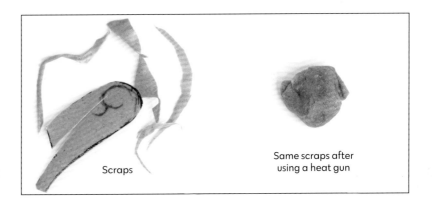

Scraps

Same scraps after using a heat gun

Methods of Construction

In its natural state, Worbla comes in rigid sheets. One side is typically very smooth, and the other has a slightly bumpy texture. When you apply heat, it becomes very malleable and adheres to many types of materials (including itself).

Worbla Options

Worbla's Finest Art, Worbla's Black Art, and Worbla's Flame Red Art are a few (but not all) of Worbla's collection of materials. It also produces a transparent version called Worbla's TranspArt, a mesh version named Worbla's Mesh Art, and a product named Kobracast Art for forming and shaping fabrics. This isn't a complete list but does include many of the materials.

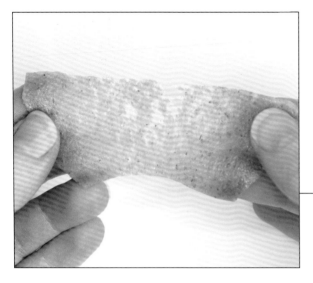

Things to Consider

- Worbla's Finest Art is the easiest type of Worbla to work with.

- Worbla becomes sticky when heated. The activation temperature is 90°C/195°F. Use a heat gun.

- When cold, Worbla is rigid. When hot, Worbla becomes malleable and can be formed and stretched.

- Overheating and stretching too much will result in the material's ripping and becoming grainy.

- For best results, work with a heat gun on the lower/slower heat setting rather than the higher/faster heat setting to avoid burning the surface.

- You can use a permanent marker like Sharpie to draw your pattern onto the surface.

- For sculpting and details, we recommend using clay sculpting tools.

- To attach two Worbla pieces together, make sure both surfaces are hot for best results.

- Avoid leaving Worbla pieces in a car or garage as pieces will bend and warp over time.

- You will be able to get fine details but will have a textured surface when you are finished.

- One side of the Worbla is shiny/smooth and the other is more matte/textured. The shiny side is a bit stickier, but when heated up, the smooth surface will become textured like the other side.

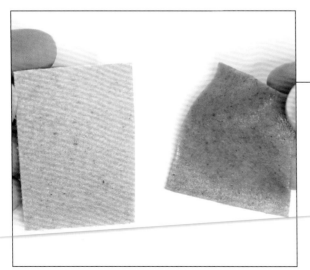

- When Worbla is heated up, it becomes slightly darker.

⚠ **SAFETY NOTE:** BE AWARE THAT IF OVERHEATED, WORBLA WILL BOND TO MOST SURFACES—INCLUDING YOUR WORK TABLE. THERMOPLASTICS MAY BE VERY HOT TO THE TOUCH WHEN HEATED. USE PROTECTIVE GLOVES OR WAIT FOR THE MATERIAL TO COOL DOWN BEFORE HANDLING.

Tiffany Gordon Cosplay

Tiffany Gordon Cosplay is a full-time cosplay builder, broadcaster, and educator teaching others how to create their own cosplays from scratch. She has been building cosplays since 2008, bringing to life her favorite characters from several anime series and video games. Tiffany is an experienced competitor, judge, convention guest, and influencer who works with several organizations and sponsors to spread her work and positivity throughout the maker community.

A

B

A | Costume ▶ Barioth Armor Set from *Monster Hunter*

Photo by Brett Downen—Downen Photography

B | Costume ▶ Mercy (Atlantic skin) from *Overwatch*

Photo by Tiffany Gordon

WRAPPING EVA FOAM WITH WORBLA

by Tiffany Gordon Cosplay

Sandwich Method Versus Covering One Side

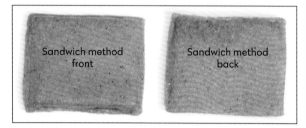

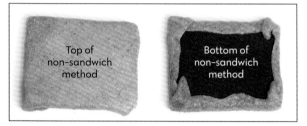

Sandwich (covering both sides in Worbla with an object inside)

- More snug final product
- Smoother/less crunchy result

/ Tip / For best results, use the sandwich method of covering.

Covering only one side in Worbla (folding the extra Worbla around the object)

- Saves time, less expensive
- Less strong
- More bendable
- More likely that the object inside will come out
- Bulkier, less smooth, more sharp edges

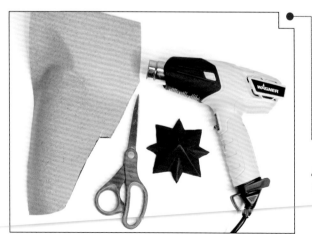

TOOLS AND MATERIALS

WORBLA

HEAT GUN

SCISSORS

EVA FOAM

UTILITY KNIFE (X-ACTO)

⚠ **SAFETY NOTE:** WHEN HEATED, WORBLA IS EXTREMELY HOT. BE CAREFUL.

Instructions

/Note/ This process will also work using Worbla's Black Art.

1 | Cut the star shape you want to wrap out of EVA foam.

2 | Cut out 2 pieces of Worbla. The first piece needs to be approximately twice as large as the EVA foam star and will act as the top shell. The second piece, which is the same size as your EVA foam piece, will act as the bottom of the shell.

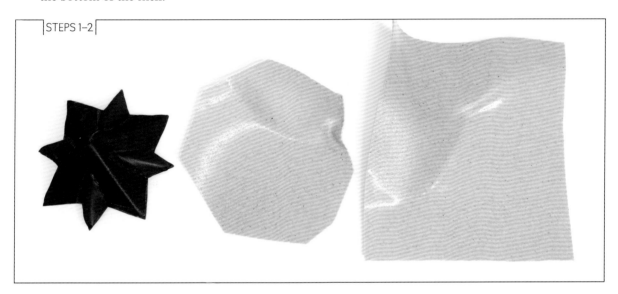

|STEPS 1–2|

3 | Using a heat gun, heat the smaller bottom piece of Worbla and affix it to the underside of your EVA foam piece.

| STEP 3 |

4 | While the smaller bottom piece is still hot, heat your larger top piece and position it over the surface of the EVA foam star. If the Worbla piece starts to get cold/stiff, apply more heat.

| Note | *If Worbla is overheated, its surface becomes grainy, and if it is stretched too fast, it can tear very easily.*

5 | Start at the top, and gently cover the surface of your EVA foam star. You want it to be as flat as possible so the Worbla will touch all edges of the star.

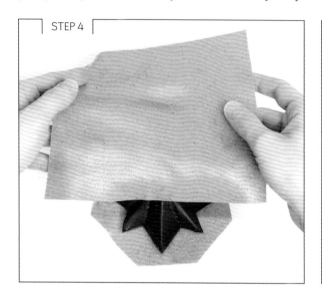

STEP 4

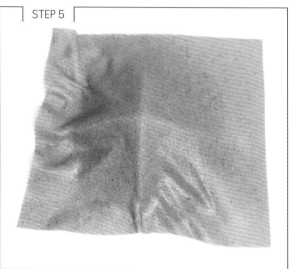

STEP 5

6 | Use your fingers to carefully and evenly press the Worbla against every edge, point, and corner of the EVA foam shape.

7 | To remove all excess Worbla, heat the edges with your heat gun, then trim using scissors, a razor blade, or a utility knife.

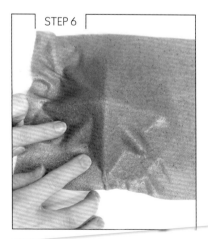

STEP 6

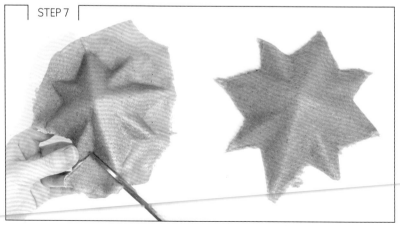

STEP 7

8 | To smooth the edges of your star, carefully heat the edges until they become soft and sculptable. Use sculpting tools to flatten and polish the edges. For deeper scratches, rips, and tears, you can use scraps of Worbla to patch and fill.

STEP 8

This technique can be used in a wide variety of ways. Good luck and have fun!

You can use this same process for the helmet for Valkyrie Mercy from the game *Overwatch*.

Costume ▸ **Mercy (Valkyrie skin)** from *Overwatch*

Photo by Tiffany Gordon Cosplay

Sayakat Cosplay

Sayakat Cosplay is an East Coast-based cosplayer from Baltimore, Maryland. She has been making her own costumes and props for more than a decade and has experience leading panels, judging cosplay contests, and running cosplay workshops. Sayakat's specialty is creating armor and props, and she loves giving back to the community by helping others to learn, producing tutorials, and attending international costume events.

B

A

A | Costume ▶ Sister of Battle from
Warhammer 40,000

Photo by S1 Price Lightworks

B | Costume ▶ Female Monk from *Diablo III*

Photo by Alexandra Lee Studios

C | Costume ▶ Maghda from *Diablo III*

Photo by Kevinertia

CREATING A FANTASY CROWN

by Sayakat Cosplay

TOOLS AND MATERIALS

WORBLA SCRAPS

HEAT GUN

PROTECTIVE GLOVES

SILICONE BAKING MAT

/ Note / I used black Worbla for this build, but you can use any type of thermoplastic.

Don't know what to do with all the Worbla scraps you've been hoarding? Use them to make headpieces, crowns, or other neat fantasy items! The great thing about a fantasy crown is that you can design and interpret it however you want! I ended up adding and subtracting some elements in the final piece versus the design that I made.

Instructions

1 | Come up with your design; it can be anything you want!

STEP 1

2 | Cut up Worbla scraps, heat them, and press them together to combine. Use a plastic container or silicone baking cup to keep the scraps organized.

3 | While the Worbla is hot, roll the combined scraps into small snakes. Use gloves to protect your hands if needed. Prepare several snakes to begin; you can always roll additional scrap snakes. Keep heating, rolling, and stretching until they are a consistent length and thickness.

STEP 2

STEP 3

4 | Heat the snakes one at a time, and manipulate them into position to match your design. Heat and combine, molding the plastic to fit the design in small sections. If it sticks to your paper, wait for the piece to cool completely before carefully peeling it from the paper. Alternatively, you can place the paper under the mat and work on top of the silicone.

5 | Continue to work in small sections, building up the piece over your pattern. Reheat pieces as necessary to ensure they are fully bonded to each other.

STEP 4

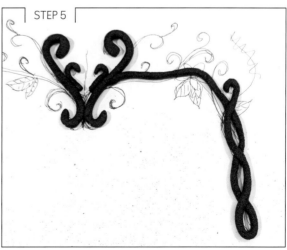

STEP 5

6 | Once the piece is complete, carefully heat small sections at a time to curve the piece. Do not heat over a Styrofoam head as it can melt the Styrofoam. Since it is a small amount of Worbla, you can use your own head as a form once the plastic has cooled a bit.

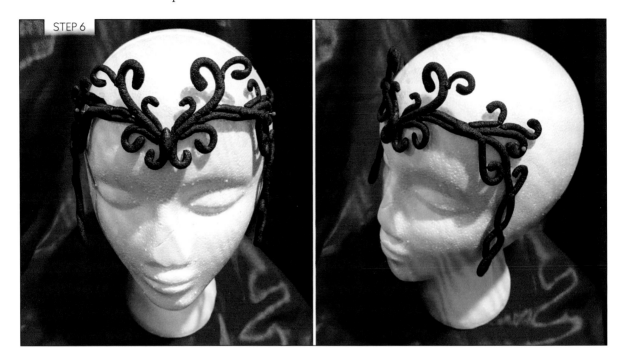

STEP 6

7 | Continue to adjust and form the overall shape of the crown.

Congrats; you are finished! Admire your work.

STEP 7

SEE MORE INFORMATION *about Tiffany Gordon Cosplay on page 11.*

WORBLA DEMO 3
MAKING A BREASTPLATE

● by Tiffany Gordon Cosplay ●

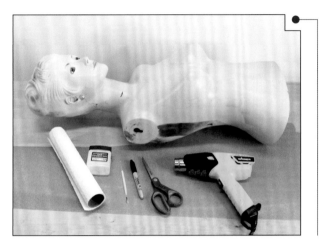

TOOLS AND MATERIALS

WORBLA'S FINEST ART

HEAT GUN

SCISSORS

FEMALE MANNEQUIN

VASELINE

PAPER TOWELS

PERMANENT MARKER LIKE SHARPIE

CLAY/SCULPTING WORKING TOOLS

WOOD GLUE

⚠ **SAFETY NOTE:** WHEN HEATED, WORBLA IS EXTREMELY HOT. BE CAREFUL.

/Note/ *I used brown Worbla for this build, but this process will work using Worbla's Black Art.*

Instructions

1 | Cut a sheet of Worbla big enough to cover the area of the mannequin from which you want to take the breastplate impression.

2 | To prevent Worbla from bonding to the mannequin, apply Vaseline with a paper towel to all surfaces that the Worbla will touch.

STEP 1

STEP 2

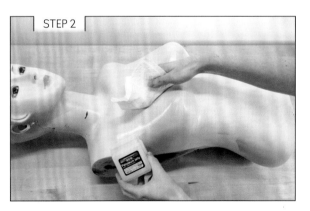

/Important!/ *Worbla is very sticky when heated. Using your heat gun too much in one area can melt not only the Worbla but also the mannequin. Try to apply heat for short periods and move around to different areas to prevent the buildup of heat and damage to your mannequin.*

3 | Position the Worbla over your mannequin, and apply heat with your heat gun in even sweeping passes. Start in the center, and work your way out.

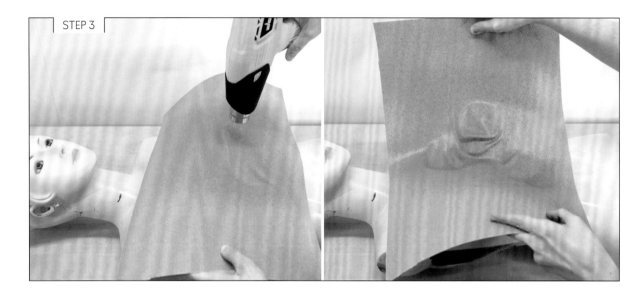

STEP 3

4 | When the Worbla is hot and malleable, it will stretch and drape over the surface. Use slight firm pressure with your fingers to reinforce the impression of the Worbla on the mannequin. Continue to smooth and polish the material by hand until you are finished. Allow this piece to completely cool and set before the next step.

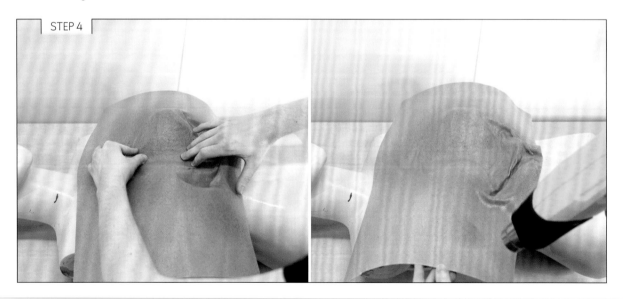

STEP 4

5 | Continue to gradually introduce heat and stretch the Worbla downward. Form the Worbla into the underside of the breast, and begin to work the surface. Use your hands again to smooth and polish the Worbla along the bottom and sides.

6 | Repeat this for the top section.

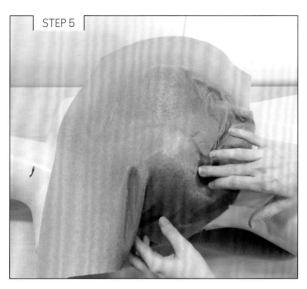

STEP 5

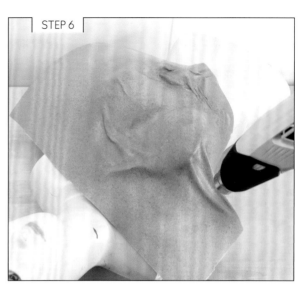

STEP 6

7 | This will then cause a single crease on the side of the breast.

8 | To remove this crease, heat the Worbla, and use scissors to cut away the excess. Apply more heat, and use a flat-headed sculpting tool to smooth and polish the seam until it has been blended. Introduce more heat if the Worbla gets too cold to sculpt.

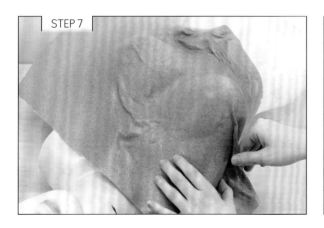

STEP 7

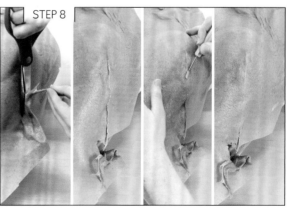

STEP 8

9 | To make the following steps easier, trim all excess Worbla from the impression with scissors.

10 | Repeat Steps 5–9 for the other side.

11 | This is what the piece should look like when finished.

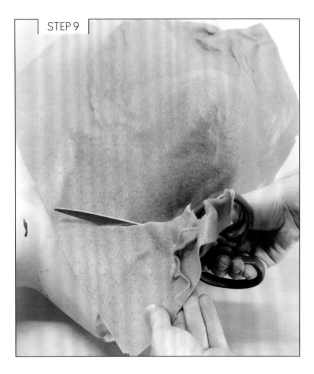

STEP 9

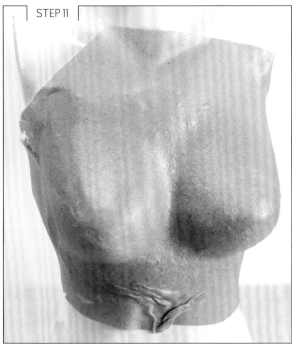

STEP 11

12 | If you have any rips or thin sections on your piece, don't worry because you can add Worbla to fix them!

STEP 12

13 | To create a Worbla patch, cut a piece large enough to cover the section you wish to patch.

14 | Heat the area to be patched as well as the patch. When ready, firmly apply the Worbla patch to make the repair. Hold the patch firmly until it has cooled down and you have completed the repair.

15 | Clean up the repair by applying heat. Use a flat-headed sculpting tool to smooth and polish the seam until it has been blended.

16 | After you have finished smoothing and repairing the Worbla, draw your intended cup design using a permanent marker like a Sharpie. Draw on any additional details you intend to add.

17 | Next, remove the Worbla from the mannequin by gently lifting it at the corners of one side. The Vaseline acts as a release agent, so it should lift easily. If it has stuck at all, move to another side, and try to lift from there. If heavy sticking occurs, you can lift from both sides in a slight twisting motion. A final trick would be to use an air hose or canned air to inject air and lift from the inside.

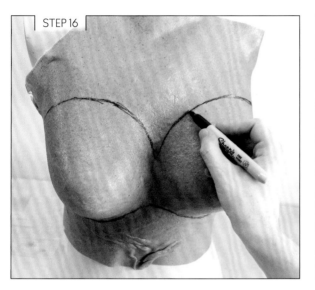

STEP 16

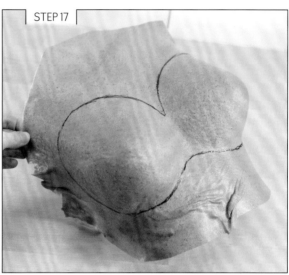

STEP 17

18 | Use scissors to cut away any extra parts of the Worbla.

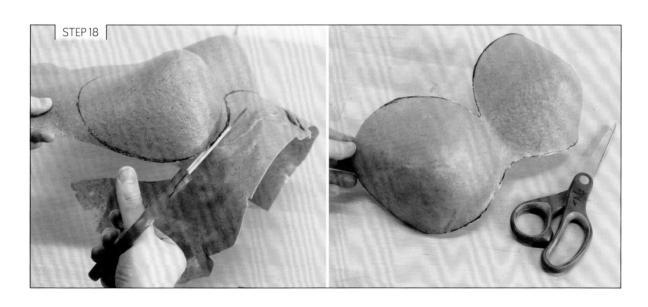

STEP 18

You are finished! At this point, you can cover your Worbla piece with leather, EVA foam, or fabric, or you can paint the Worbla.

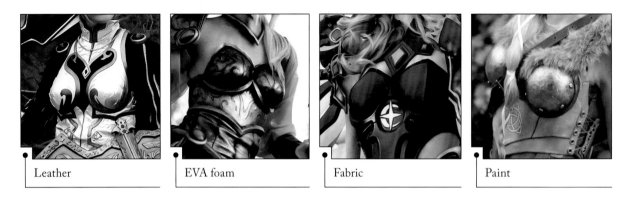

Leather   EVA foam   Fabric   Paint

Worbla has a grainy surface texture. To smooth this out, apply several coats of wood glue over the entire surface. You will want to build up 1 to 3 coats until you reach your desired level of smoothness. Allow each coat to dry for 24 hours before applying the next coat.

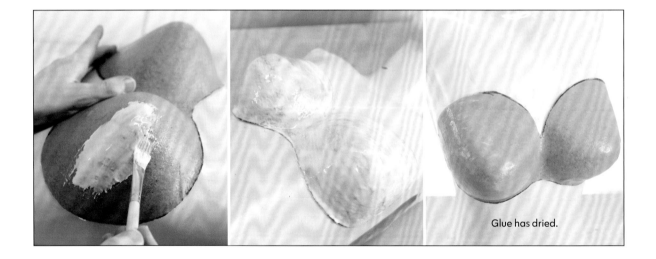

Glue has dried.

Sameer Tikka Masala

Sameer Tikka Masala (Sameer Bundela) is a pioneering cosplayer from India, having the honor of being the first professional cosplayer from his home country and winning the title of Indian Champion of Cosplay four times. He regularly takes workshops in some of the biggest colleges and conventions in India and has given a TED talk on the subject. Sameer also has the distinction of being the first cosplayer from India to win an international cosplay competition and has represented the country at many international events. Sameer runs his own business as a freelance artist and art director focusing on design and fabrication of all kinds of props, costumes, display pieces, and more for movies, TV shows, events, and commission work.

Costume ▶ Ares from *Smite*

Photos by Sameer Tikka Masala

Sameer Tikka Masala,
COSPLAYER

Costume ▸ **Jamie Lannister**
from *Game of Thrones*

Photo by Yash Indap

Photo by Ultimate Cosplay

CREATING RELIEFS

● by Sameer Tikka Masala ●

This demonstration is meant to show you how you can use Worbla to make intricate relief work, which can then be used for a multitude of purposes such as decorations for cosplay armor, cards, book covers, and wall displays.

TOOLS AND MATERIALS

WORBLA PEARLY ART

SCISSORS

SCULPTING TOOLS

ALUMINUM OR ARMATURE WIRE

ALUMINUM FOIL OR FOAM CLAY

HEAT GUN

KRAZY GLUE OR SUPER GLUE

SILICONE MAT

PENCIL OR PEN

PAPER

PAPER TAPE

TWEEZERS

/ Worbla Note / Although Worbla Pearly Art is used in this demo, you can use the techniques learned in this chapter for other types of Worbla or other similar thermoplastics.

/ Sculpting with Worbla Note / For this demo, an additive sculpting technique is being utilized, which is achieved by building up single layers of Worbla as you continue to sculpt. Although it is possible to heat a large portion of Worbla and simply cut off any excess, because of its adhesive properties, this alternative method can be messy and has the potential to damage any intricate designs you may have already sculpted.

Instructions

1 | On paper, draw the design you plan to sculpt.

/Tip/ You can print your reference if you're basing your design on existing intellectual property. Just be sure that you print it true to size.

/Note/ While you can sculpt without Step 1, having a reference, no matter how basic, is very useful and highly recommended. Having this will help you plan out your layers as you work and help prevent backtracking. It will also help you maintain proportions, especially for organic objects and creatures.

2 | Analyze your reference to identify which section will serve as your base. This tends to be the bottommost layer, and it will be on the bulkier side. For the dragon in this demo, the base will be the body. Using your aluminum foil or foam clay, start sculpting your base layer. This doesn't need to be super accurate, but try to maintain thickness and make it as dense as possible.

/Tip/ You'll be pressing your Worbla into this base piece next, so make your piece thick enough so it will not collapse under that pressure.

/Note/ Although you can use Worbla for this base piece, it would be a waste of material and would add unnecessary weight to your piece.

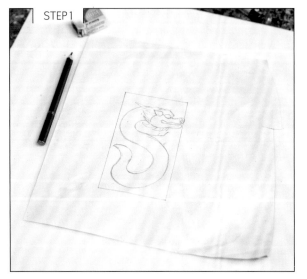

STEP 1

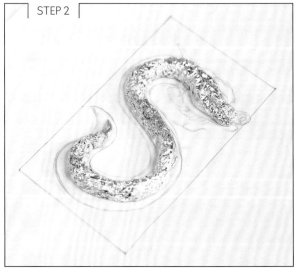

STEP 2

3 | Place your newly sculpted base onto the Worbla and trace it, leaving enough of a seam allowance to cover the entire piece. Once you're done, cut it out with scissors.

/Tip/ The thicker the shape, the more seam allowance you'll need!

STEP 3

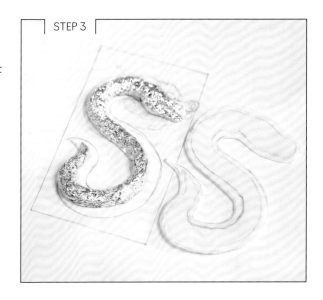

4 | Working over the silicone mat, use a heat gun on your Worbla piece until it gets soft, and start bending it along the shape of your base sculpture. Once you're satisfied with the placement, begin heating smaller sections of Worbla, and wrap them around the curves of your base with a sculpting tool. Once that is done, create a seam for the head and mouth by gently pressing in the area with a thinner tool.

STEP 4

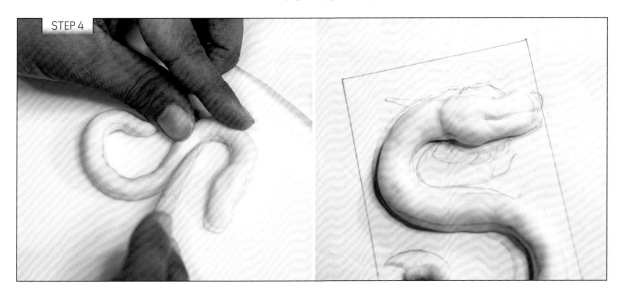

5 | For the next layer, cut out another piece of Worbla by repeating Step 3, but this time stop at the neck. Repeat Step 4, and wrap this new layer over the previous one.

/ Note / *It is possible to start sculpting your details on the first layer. Heat wrapping Worbla reduces its thickness and could cause tearing. Double layering creates a thick and sturdy base that produces a smoother and more consistent surface.*

6 | With a pencil, draw on any details you want to sculpt on the body. For the example in this demo, those details are the scales and the ribbed design on the belly.

/Note/ *You want to start with the main body because the head details are more delicate and can be damaged as you sculpt.*

STEP 6

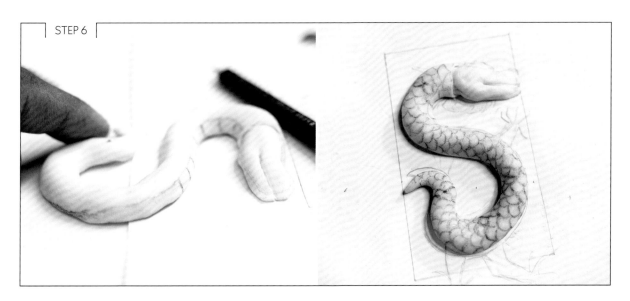

7 | With a flat, thin sculpting tool, begin to press in the details you drew for Step 6. Heat the section accordingly; shallower grooves like the scales will require less heat compared to the deeper crease for the mouth.

/Note/ *Don't press too hard, as the Worbla layers can still rip or tear if too much pressure is applied.*

STEP 7

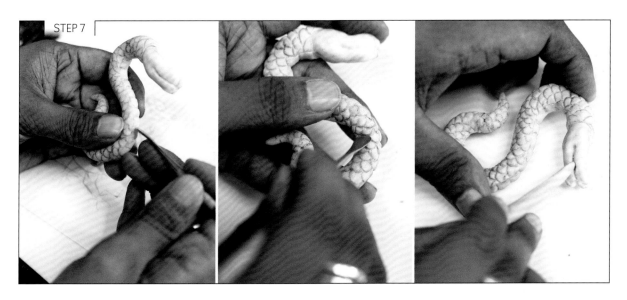

8 | Now start to build the definition on the head. Heat scrap pieces of Worbla into a lump. Pull a small lump out of the larger one, and create the forehead of the dragon. Keep checking the proportions of your piece by transposing it on top of your drawing periodically. Merge the pieces by pressing with a blunt tool on the joining edge. Create a cavity for the eye socket, and insert a small lump for the eye.

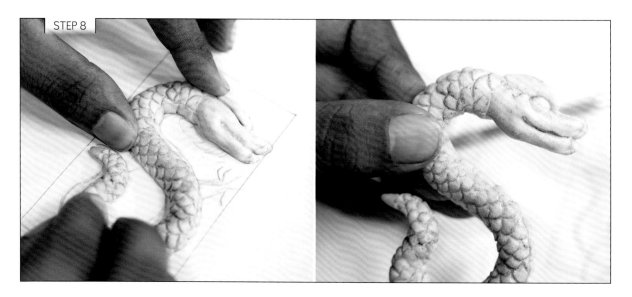

9 | Repeat Step 8 to create the different details on the head such as the chin, nose, horns, ears, and beard tendrils until you're satisfied with how it looks. Track the order in which you place them, remembering to go from bottom to top.

/ Note / *Heating small pieces of Worbla can get tricky, so a good trick is to stick a small piece of tape on your desk with the glue side up and place your small bit on it before heating so the piece doesn't fly off.*

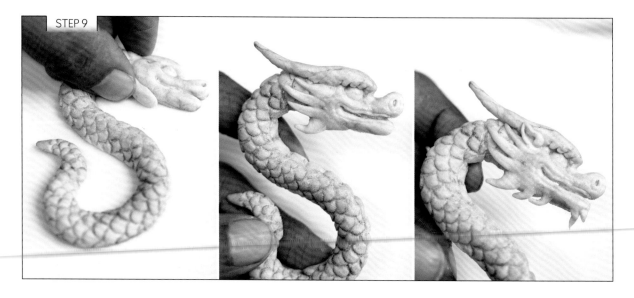

10 | Create all the small details like lips, eyebrows, nostrils, and ear lobes by following Step 7.

11 | To give your dragon a cute mustache, roll a long, thin piece of Worbla. The Worbla mustache should maintain its shape, but if you're finding it difficult to maintain a specific shape without bending it, you can reinforce it by embedding a thin wire inside. Be sure to heat only the areas that you intend to attach.

STEP 11

12 | Create another long and thin strip of Worbla; cut out triangles for the dorsal fins.

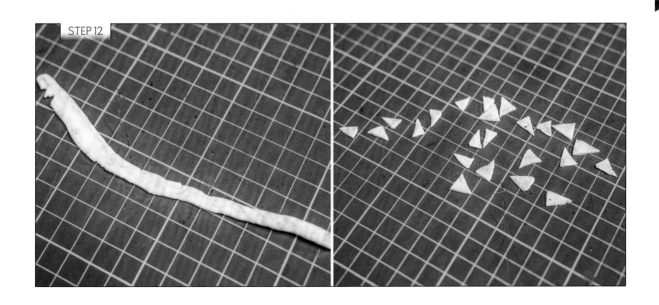

STEP 12

13 | Heat individual fins while holding them with tweezers, and embed the fins into the body. You can sculpt an organic shape with your hands or with tools after embedding them.

/ Tip / *You might need to use the glue of your choice if the pieces are not staying on the body. Slightly overlap each fin with the last, and merge them to make them look more organic.*

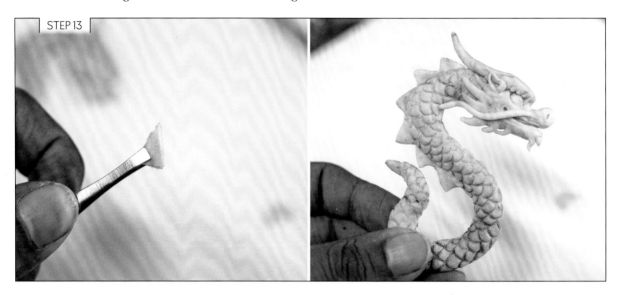

STEP 13

14 | Place your creation next to your design, and feel amazing!

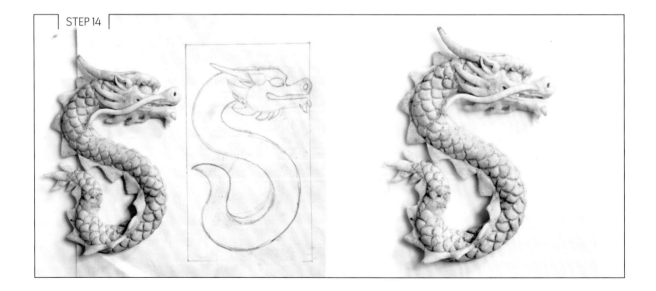

STEP 14

We're finished!

Unless you want a buttery-smooth surface, in which case you'd need to prime and sand it a few times (I didn't), you can jump straight to painting it.

I wanted mine to look like a cool dragon sigil. Now I can stick it on top of any armor piece or book cover, make a pin out of it, or even create a whole diorama around it! The possibilities are endless! You can use this process of thinking and steps to create almost any creature or organic detail. Get sculpting!

Panterona Cosplay

Panterona Cosplay is an award-winning cosplayer, fashion designer, and convention organizer from the Caribbean Island of Trinidad and Tobago. She has been actively cosplaying since 2005; has created a wide variety of characters from anime, comics, cartoons, and games; and has won awards in several countries. Panterona is also an experienced judge and cosplay guest, having worked shows in the Caribbean, United States, Italy, United Kingdom, Canada, and Japan!

A

B

C

A | Costume ▶ Original Fae Character

Photo by GK Studios

B | Costume ▶ Fran from *Final Fantasy XII*

Photo by GK Studios

C | Costume ▶ Gamora from *Guardians of the Galaxy*

Photo by Gareth Leigh Photography

CREATING A GEM AND LIGHTING PANEL

by Panterona Cosplay

This demonstration will teach you how to create gems/lighting panels for cosplay using Worbla's TranspArt. These gems are incredibly lightweight and can be used on costumes or props that need larger gems but that need to be very light! The technique comes in handy for people without access to resin casting materials and for those who live in small apartments/enclosed areas where the fumes from those materials would be problematic.

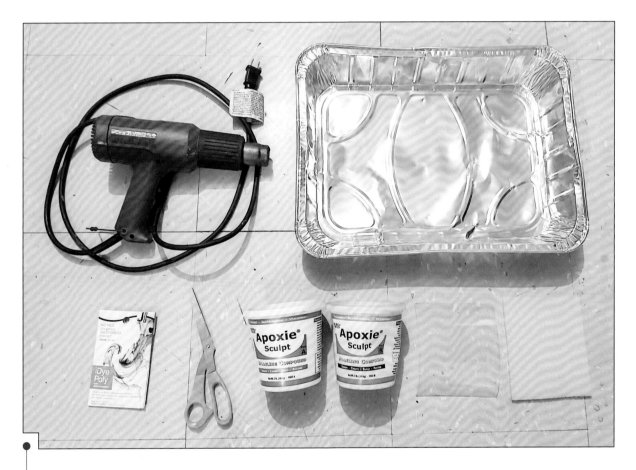

TOOLS AND MATERIALS

SHEET OF WORBLA'S TRANSPART

HEAT GUN

CLAY OR APOXIE SCULPT

1 PACKET OF IDYE POLY IN YOUR COLOR OF CHOICE

THIN UPHOLSTERY FOAM OR FABRIC OF CHOICE (OPTIONAL)

SCISSORS

STAINLESS STEEL, ALUMINUM, OR ENAMEL POT/TRAY

RELEASE AGENT (OPTIONAL)

⚠ **SAFETY NOTE:** THERMOPLASTICS MAY BE VERY HOT TO THE TOUCH WHEN HEATED. USE PROTECTIVE GLOVES.

Instructions

1 | Create/sculpt the design for your positive mold. This can be as simple or complex as your project requires. For simplicity, we will be creating a gem shaped like a circular cabochon in this tutorial.

/ Pro Tip! / You can make your mold any shape/size you want. I used this technique to create large lighting panels for my Elisabeth cosplay, for example (see photos).

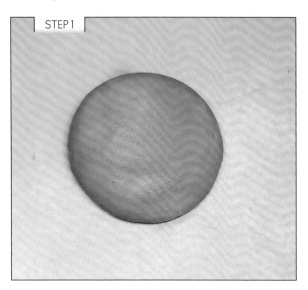

STEP 1

2 | Prepare your Worbla for heat forming! You can dye it any color you want using iDye Poly by following the directions on the packet. Place the dye into boiling water, stir, and submerge your sheet of Worbla until it reaches the desired color. Make sure to wash the Worbla first to ensure the dye permeates evenly, and be sure to wash it after to get rid of any dye residue.

For dyeing thermoplastics generally, check out the tutorial by Hoku Props on page 148.

⚠ **SAFETY NOTE:** UTENSILS AND POT/TRAY USED FOR DYEING SHOULD NOT BE USED FOR FOOD.

STEP 2

3 | Once your Worbla is the color desired, cut out an adequately sized piece that is roughly bigger than your mold. If this is your first time working with this material, be sure to give yourself more than enough allowance; that is, do not cut your pieces too small.

4 | Apply a release agent to your mold. This can be something as simple as a thin layer of Vaseline or hand cream. While not completely necessary because of the nature of the mold, it can help in separating the Worbla once it has cooled.

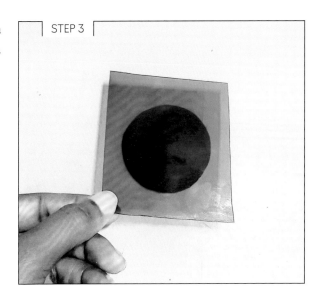

STEP 3

5 | Place your Worbla over the mold, and start applying heat in a circular motion from the middle of your mold outward. You want to ensure that it is heated evenly so that when you start stretching the Worbla over the mold it offers the least resistance.

/ Pro Tip! / *I would advise working on a test piece first to get a handle on the heat settings that work best for your heat gun with this Worbla type and the distance from the Worbla needed to properly activate it. If bubbles start forming, you have overheated/burned it. But that can be a cool effect depending on the look you are going for. For example, I purposefully burned the Worbla for the gems in my Neptulon cosplay to give it more of a water/bubble effect! See below.*

STEP 5

6 | Take your time, and stretch the Worbla evenly over the mold. For bigger molds, you will have to do this in parts, but for small gems like these, I can usually get it done in one go.

STEP 6

7 | Once the mold is completely covered, wait for the Worbla to cool before trimming away the excess and removing the Worbla from the mold. You should now have a cute Worbla gem cover!

8 | You can use this as is, or you can opt to add some depth to it by inserting upholstery foam in the color of your choice inside of it!

You can also add LEDs to the inside of these gems, with the upholstery foam acting as a light diffuser! The sky is the limit! Play around with different material inserts like fabric and glitter for different effects!

And you are finished! Now attach your lightweight gems or lighting panels to your costume/prop! I hope you found this tutorial helpful! Feel free to tag me in any projects using this technique!

STEP 7

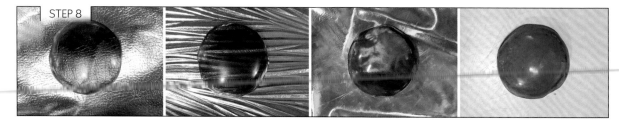

STEP 8

CREATING CLEAR POLYGONAL SHAPES WITH TranspArt

by Tiffany Gordon Cosplay

SEE MORE INFORMATION *about Tiffany Gordon Cosplay on page 11.*

About TranspArt (Clear Worbla)

- This is the most difficult of the types of Worbla to work with but is well worth the effort.

- It activates at 120°C/250°F, which is higher than the other types of Worbla. Use a heat gun.

- TranspArt does not adhere to itself.

- Leaving it in your car or garage during summer is not recommended as your pieces may warp or come apart.

- Closed objects, such as cubes, will expand in the heat, and some seams may separate. You can fix them the same way you assemble them.

- When cold, the material is hard. When hot/heated, it becomes pliable enough to make into the form that you want. While hot/heated, it becomes a bit sticky, so be careful with your surface table or what you are molding it over as it may stick to the surface.

- Try to not overheat the clear Worbla as it will turn a milky-white color rather than being transparent, and it will get bubbles.

- Cut pieces with scissors.

- Score pieces with utility knife to bend.

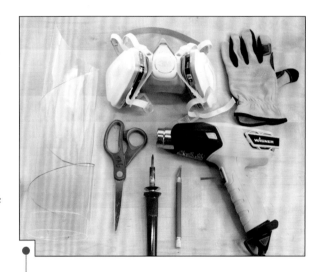

TOOLS AND MATERIALS

HEAT GUN

SOLDERING IRON WITH FLAT TIP

SCISSORS

UTILITY KNIFE (X-ACTO)

SAFETY RESPIRATOR (SOLDERING IRON WILL MELT THE WORBLA, CREATING FUMES YOU DO NOT WANT TO INHALE)

SAFETY GLASSES OR SAFETY GOGGLES (SOLDERING IRON MELTS WORBLA, CAUSING SMOKE TO RISE AND IRRITATE THE EYES)

HEAT-RESISTANT GLOVES

WELL-VENTILATED AREA

Over time, the soldering iron will turn black from the heat, and this will cause discoloration to the clear Worbla, turning it black where the iron touches. Clean the soldering iron regularly to avoid this. You can do it by unplugging the soldering iron and using a utility knife to scrape down/away from you, scraping the black soot off of the soldering iron. You can use a wire cleaning brush to do the same thing.

⚠ **SAFETY NOTE:** ALWAYS BE SURE TO WEAR SAFETY GLASSES AND A RESPIRATOR.

Instructions

1 | Draw a pattern on paper. Place your pattern under the Worbla, and trace the pattern onto the Worbla using a permanent marker like a Sharpie.

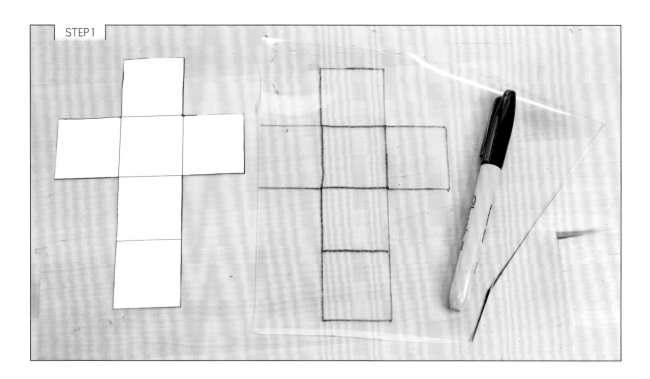

2 | Cut out the Worbla with scissors along the outer perimeter of the pattern.

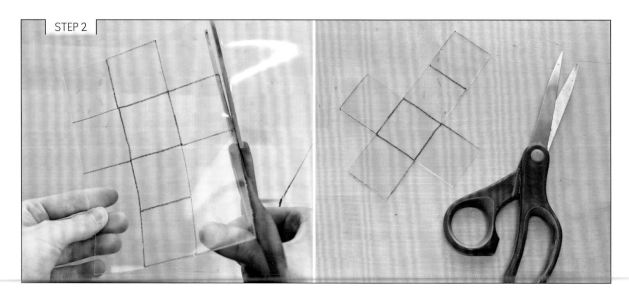

3 | Score the inner pattern lines, using a ruler as a guide and very lightly running your razor blade or X-ACTO knife along the surface of the Worbla.

4 | Carefully bend the pieces along the score lines until they are at a 90° (square) angle.

⚠ **SAFETY NOTE:** THE NEXT STEP REQUIRES ALL SAFETY EQUIPMENT (PERSONAL PROTECTIVE EQUIPMENT), INCLUDING SAFETY GLASSES, A RESPIRATOR WITH VOC CANISTERS, AND HEAT-RESISTANT GLOVES. ENSURE YOU ARE WORKING IN A WELL-VENTILATED AREA.

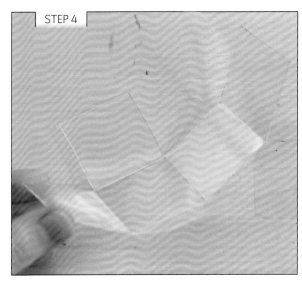
STEP 4

5 | Using the flat side of a soldering iron, slowly run the hot blade along the seam to weld the edges together. Apply slight pressure to ensure the gap is tight enough to weld. Maintain pressure until the joints cool and set.

6 | Repeat Step 5 until all desired edges have been welded together.

STEP 5

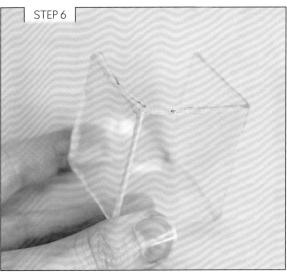
STEP 6

You can use this same process for the crystal tail for K/DA Ahri from the game *League of Legends*.

Tiffany Gordon,
COSPLAYER

Costume ▶ K/DA Ahri from
League of Legends

Photos by Tiffany Gordon

Wonderflex

What Is Wonderflex?

Wonderflex is an extruded composite thermoplastic sheet that will soften into a pliable and moldable material that is great to use in cosplay for more rigid crafting purposes.

Uses

Wonderflex is great for creating full props and details or even forming positive or negative molds.

Methods of Construction

Wonderflex becomes malleable when heat is applied to it. It can be cut with hand tools such as scissors and knives.

Wonderflex Options

Wonderflex Original: This is another product thought of as a traditional thermoplastic as it is hard and rigid at room temperature. To shape, warp, and work with it, you just need to apply heat. This thin-but-dense plastic has a thin sheet of textile mesh running through it, which helps to keep it from melting apart when it gets too hot. One side is smooth, and the other has a grippy mesh feel.

Wonderflex Pro: This is a modernization of Wonderflex Original and does not have any mesh textile in its makeup. It is perfectly smooth on both sides and is great for creating full props and details or even forming positive or negative molds. Also rigid at room temperature, it can be formed by applying heat. It is very similar to Thibra (page 60) in many respects.

Things to Consider

Due to the mesh textile in Wonderflex Original, it is often beneficial to use Wonderflex as a core layer when sandwiching different thermoplastics together into a composite. This also resolves any potential issue with the surface finish.

⚠️ **SAFETY NOTE:** THERMOPLASTICS MAY BE VERY HOT TO THE TOUCH WHEN HEATED. USE PROTECTIVE GLOVES OR WAIT FOR THE MATERIAL TO COOL BEFORE HANDLING.

Tock Custom

Christopher Tock is a self-taught tailor and cosplayer from Milwaukee, Wisconsin. In 2015 he founded Tock Custom as a clothing brand, taking custom commission work, and started teaching sewing and cosplay programming. Tock is an experienced competitive cosplayer, contest judge, event host, organizer, and instructor and is sponsored by several creative industry brand names. In 2020, Tock cofounded Ultimate Cosplay, alongside Hoku Props, to facilitate high-production community cosplay events, competitions, and other programming.

B

A

A | Costume ▶ **Zinogre Blademaster from** *Monster Hunter*

Photo by Brett Downen—Downen Photography

B | Costume ▶ **Edward Elric from** *Fullmetal Alchemist*

Photo by Photo Persuasion

C | Costume ▶ **Lothar from** *World of Warcraft*

Photo by Alexandra Lee Studios

C

CREATING TEXTURED COSPLAY HORNS

by Tock Custom

This demonstration showcases how to detail EVA foam horns using both Worbla and Wonderflex to achieve different finishing textures. This technique is also a great way to create accents with a very rigid surface.

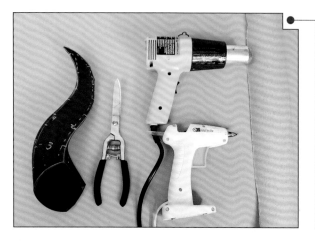

TOOLS AND MATERIALS

HANDMADE EVA FOAM HORNS

4MM EVA FOAM

HORN PATTERNS BY KAMUI COSPLAY

SMALL SHEET OF WORBLA (WORBLA'S FINEST ART)

SHEET OF WONDERFLEX

SCISSORS (HEAVY-DUTY SHEARS BY FAMORÉ CUTLERY)

HEAT GUN

HOT GLUE (IN CASE THE MATERIAL DOESN'T STICK)

⚠ **SAFETY NOTE:** THERMOPLASTICS MAY BE VERY HOT TO THE TOUCH WHEN HEATED. USE PROTECTIVE GLOVES OR WAIT FOR THE MATERIAL TO COOL DOWN BEFORE HANDLING.

TECHNIQUE NUMBER 1

RIBBED HORNS WITH WONDERFLEX—KAMUI COSPLAY "CURVED HORNS" PATTERN

Instructions

1 | Assemble horns or accessories using EVA foam. Use any pattern you'd like to modify and texture.

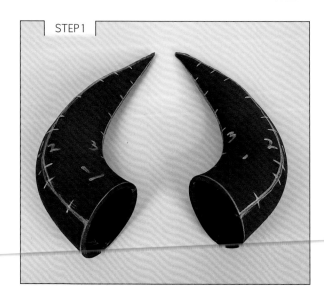

STEP 1

2 | With your scissors, cut out long, ½″ strips of Wonderflex to prepare the ribs.

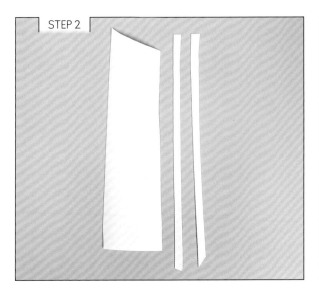

STEP 2

3 | Heat your strips using your heat gun until they become malleable before rolling them along a hard surface to form thin, round dowels.

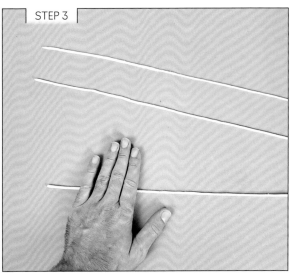

STEP 3

4 | Reheat your first dowel with your heat gun, and wrap it around your horn as desired. Cut the dowel where it meets after each full wrap. Heat the Wonderflex ends again to stick them together. Repeat this process until you're happy with the coverage on your horn.

5 | While adding a slight seam allowance to account for the EVA foam thickness, trace the same pattern used to make your base horns onto your Wonderflex sheet with the mesh side down. Cut out the pieces.

STEP 4

6 | Heat the bottom of your center panel, and attach the corresponding edge to the bottom of your horn.

STEP 6

7 | Slowly heat the Wonderflex while affixing it to your horn and over each rib until you reach the tip. Repeat this process with your remaining pattern pieces.

/Tip/ *If there are any gaps, you can cover them up with smaller pieces of Wonderflex.*

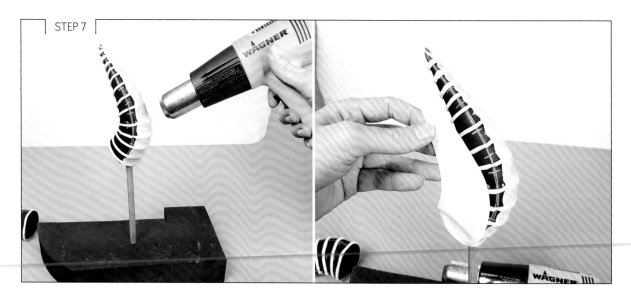

STEP 7

8 | If needed, apply heat to each panel, and press the Wonderflex deeper into the ribs to create more depth and texture.

You're all finished! Now is the time to attach the horns to your armor, headband, or helmet. Be aware that these materials will add a bit of weight, so plan for a robust method of attaching your new accents.

STEP 8

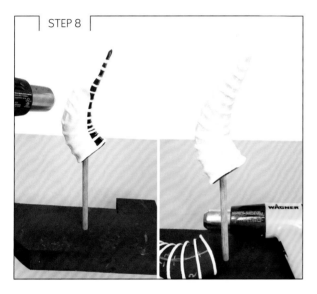

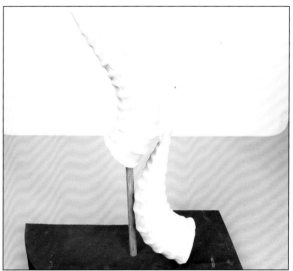

TECHNIQUE NUMBER 2
SPIRALED HORNS WITH WORBLA—KAMUI COSPLAY "LONG HORNS" PATTERN

Instructions

1 | Assemble horns or accessories using EVA foam. Use any pattern you'd like to modify and texture.

2 | Use your scissors to cut a 1″ circle out of Worbla or Wonderflex. Apply heat with your heat gun before wrapping this piece around the tip of your horn.

STEP 1

STEP 2

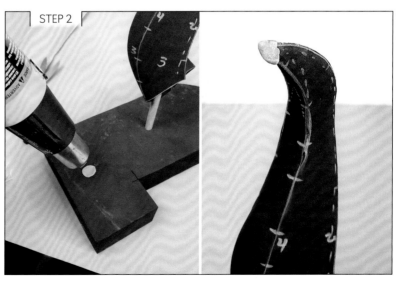

3 | Cut out long strips of your thermoplastic of choice, and use your scissors again to cut one side into a jagged edge. For the top part of each horn, the strip was about 1˝ wide; for the bottom of each horn, the material was cut about 2˝ wide.

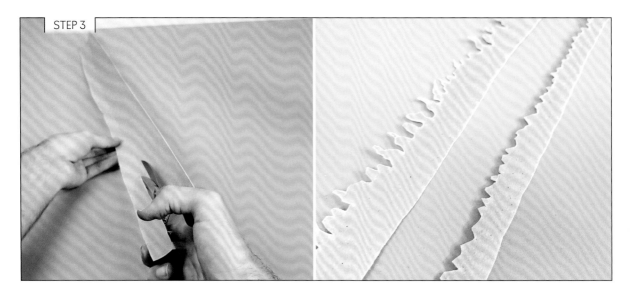

STEP 3

4 | Apply heat to one end of your prepared strips. Then carefully press the heated end into the tip of your horn so that it slightly covers the material on the top. Start slowly wrapping your thermoplastic around your prop in a spiral manner, applying heat as needed.

| Note | Both Worbla and Wonderflex will adhere to themselves when heated, so you may not need any hot glue or contact cement at all.

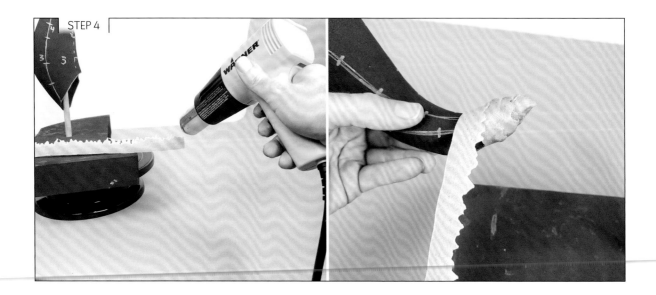

STEP 4

5 | As you get closer to the bottom, feel free to use a wider strip of material to give it a great organic look.

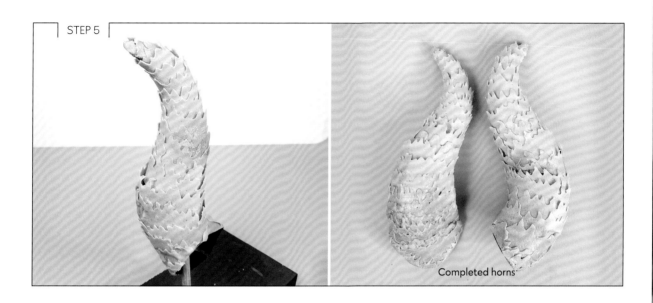

STEP 5

Completed horns

6 | As you reach the bottom of your horns, you may leave about a ½″ of material to heat and wrap around the bottom edge of your prop.

You're all finished! Now is the time to attach the horns to your armor, headband, or helmet. Be aware that these materials will add a bit of weight, so plan for a robust method of attaching your new accents.

Now that you're finished, feel free to prime, paint, weather, and seal your accessories as desired.

STEP 6

SEE MORE
INFORMATION
*about Tock Custom
on page 48.*

WONDERFLEX DEMO 2
CREATING LAYERED ARMOR

● by Tock Custom ●

This demonstration showcases how to create scaled armor with pivoting joints using Wonderflex (or your thermoplastic of choice). These techniques can be used to create scaled armor for arms, legs, shoulders, and more!

TOOLS AND MATERIALS

WONDERFLEX OR FORMABLE PLASTIC OF YOUR CHOICE

MASKING TAPE

PENS AND MARKERS

4MM OR 6MM CHICAGO SCREWS

SCISSORS

ROTATING HOLE PUNCH TOOL

HEAT GUN

⚠ **SAFETY NOTE:** THERMOPLASTICS MAY BE VERY HOT TO THE TOUCH WHEN HEATED. USE PROTECTIVE GLOVES OR WAIT FOR THE MATERIAL TO COOL DOWN BEFORE HANDLING.

/Note / *In this demonstration, I created a copy of my lower left leg out of EVA foam (you could use a mannequin or body form). This was my reference for making patterns for our new scaled armor panel.*

Instructions

1 | Apply masking tape to the body form. Starting on the left side, work your way across using long strips of tape until the entire area is covered. It's helpful to overlap the tape by about half the width so it all comes off in one piece.

STEP 1

2 | Draw a centerline and side guides to your body form to help center your patterns. Then, start planning and sketching the shape of each scale.

3 | When you're happy with the look, finish everything over in marker, and number each part.

4 | After you have all your lines drawn, carefully remove the tape from your reference. Take your time, and make sure the patterns don't tear.

STEP 2

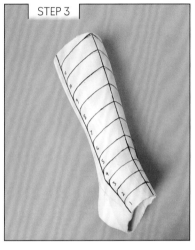

STEP 3

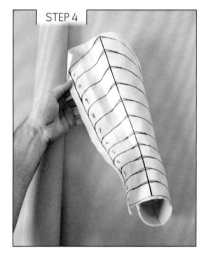

STEP 4

5 | Transfer the sketch to paper to create the final pattern. To avoid puckering, cut the masking tape sketch into sections so it will lay flat on the paper. Stick the tape to a sheet of paper, and then cut out each independent part.

6 | For the final prop to articulate properly, add an overlap allowance for the joints. In this case, I added a ½″ allowance to the bottom of each scale. This will give plenty of room to punch Chicago screws and material coverage when the joints pivot.

7 | Trace the final pattern onto your material and cut it out. Make sure you transfer the pattern to the right side of your material, or it will be backward. Here you can see the draft pattern, the final pattern, and the materials all cut out.

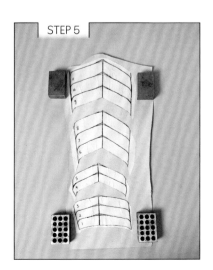

STEP 5

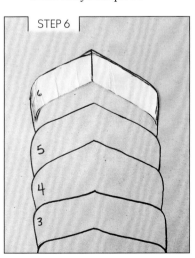

STEP 6

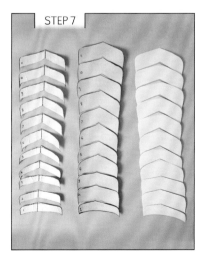

STEP 7

8 | Start heat forming all your scales. It is helpful to trace the shape of each scale to your form to get a perfect fit. Center each scale on your dress form, and apply heat with a heat gun until it drapes over from side to side.

9 | Smooth out the material to make sure there are no bubbles or puckers in your scales. The material may be very hot, so be careful here. Once it cools, it will become rigid, and you can pop it off.

/Note/ *You must do one scale at a time. If you stack scales when heat forming, they will fuse together, and you will not be able to separate them.*

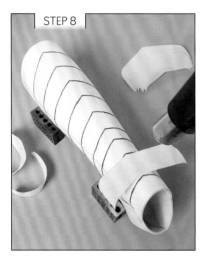

STEP 8

STEP 9

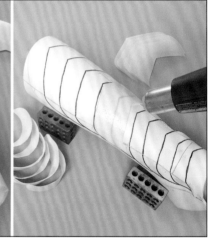

10 | It's time to assemble your scales! Line up each overlap of scales, and punch a hole using your punch tool. Now would be the best time to prime and paint your scales before assembly.

11 | Simply insert the female part of each screw into each joint on either side, and make sure they pivot properly. Chicago screws are fantastic in cosplay as they give the appearance of rivets but allow smooth movement.

STEP 10

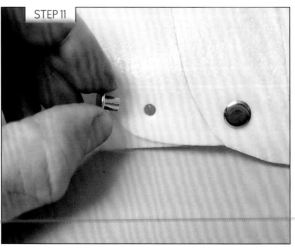

STEP 11

12 | On the inside of your armor, screw in the male sides of the screws to secure each scale.

STEP 12

This type of armor lends itself very well to adding fittings. You could easily secure a few scraps of leather and some buckles right into the Chicago screws! You could use hook-and-loop tape, elastic, or fabric for fittings as well.

That'll do it; you should now have some great wearable armor that is comfortable and rigid! If you haven't painted yet, disassemble everything and use your favorite metallic paints and a high-gloss topcoat to make it look like real metal. Then just put it back together and you're good to go!

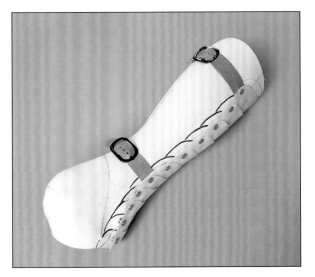

Thibra

What Is Thibra?

Thibra Tex is a sculptable plastic reinforced with mesh webbing. It is perfect for large projects requiring structure and stability. Thibra Fine is a sculptable plastic with excellent properties for sculpting extra-fine details. It is reusable, nontoxic, and biodegradable, making it an eco-friendly cosplay material option. Thibra is smooth on both sides, stays firm in its natural state, and is extremely versatile when heat is added.

Uses

Thibra is a thermoplastic material that can be used to create costume pieces, masks, or even harnesses. Scraps can be used to make smaller detailed pieces, and because they can adhere to practically any surface, they can be combined with other materials.

Methods of Construction

Thibra can be sculpted into objects or molded; you can use it to create armor, props, or accents that can be added to just about anything.

Thibra Options

Thibra Fine is smooth, malleable, and biodegradable and can be heated to create double-curved shapes, sphere shapes, and other extreme forms. Once cooled, you can reheat it as needed to make corrections.

Thibra Tex is blue and has a mesh reinforcement layer for larger pieces. It is more resilient and durable than Thibra Fine and ideal as a base layer for large projects; it is not quite as smooth as Thibra Fine. Sheets are more than 1mm thick. Sheets can be loosely rolled, cut with standard scissors or paper cutters, and heated with either hot water or a heat gun.

Things to Consider

- Because Thibra will stick to most surfaces, always work on a nonstick Teflon or silicone sheet.

- Hot Thibra will stick to latex or nitrile gloves and some thermal gloves, depending on the material.

- Thibra can be bent while cool, but the bending can stress and weaken the material.

⚠ **SAFETY NOTE:** THERMOPLASTICS MAY BE VERY HOT TO THE TOUCH WHEN HEATED. USE PROTECTIVE GLOVES OR WAIT FOR THE MATERIAL TO COOL DOWN BEFORE HANDLING.

Photo by Alkali

Alkali

Alkali is a fantastic costume designer from Boise, Idaho. She got her start in cosplay after appearing at a convention as a special effects makeup artist, where her work and her hand-made costumes made headlines! She has experience working in short films and commercials as well as guesting at conventions, judging, and community building for the gaming industry. Alkali works for a well-known game developer and is always lending her expertise to cosplay conventions around the world.

Costume Valeera Sanguinar from *World of Warcraft*

Photo by Brett Downen—Downen Photography

BUILDING STRUCTURED SHAPES WITH THIBRA TEX

by Alkali

This demo will showcase Thibra Tex as a base for structured corset boning in a high-fantasy elf corset.

TOOLS AND MATERIALS

THIBRA TEX

SILICONE MAT

HEAT GUN

PLASTIC MANNEQUIN

CLEAR ACRYLIC RULER

MASKING TAPE

SCISSORS

WHITE MAKEUP EYE PENCIL

THIN SHARPIE OR PERMANENT MARKER

14 SMALL D-RINGS

⚠ **SAFETY NOTE:** THERMOPLASTICS MAY BE VERY HOT TO THE TOUCH WHEN HEATED. USE PROTECTIVE GLOVES OR WAIT FOR THE MATERIAL TO COOL DOWN BEFORE HANDLING.

Instructions

1 | Use your white makeup eye pencil to sketch your design on the plastic mannequin.

2 | With your Sharpie and ruler, trace 20 strips 14″ × ¼″ onto your Thibra.

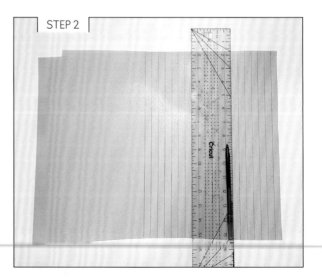

STEP 1

STEP 2

3 | Cut out the strips of Thibra using your scissors.

4 | Hold up a Thibra strip, and use your Sharpie to mark the length needed to fit your design before using scissors to cut the excess length.

/Tip/ Err on the side of caution by leaving a little excess length. It's easier to cut away material than it is to add!

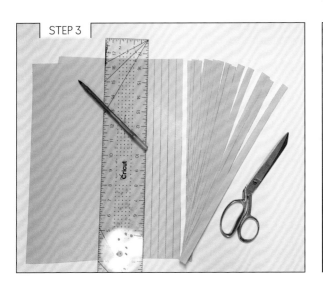

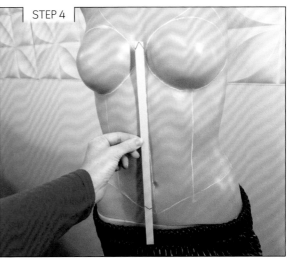

5 | Place the strip of Thibra you just cut onto your silicone mat with the mesh side up. Set your heat gun on a low setting, and move it over the Thibra until it becomes malleable.

6 | Heated strips can be placed on your mannequin mesh side down. The strips will stick to the surface of the mannequin but can be pulled off easily later.

/Note/ As you handle the mannequin and add more strips, the Thibra is susceptible to losing adhesion. Use masking tape to help stabilize the strips if needed.

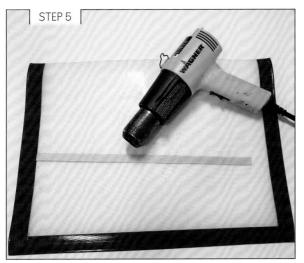

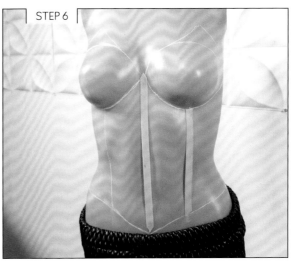

7 | Using what you learned in Steps 3–6, continue placing Thibra strips onto your mannequin over your white guidelines.

/Tip / *Remember to place your strips mesh side down!*

8 | After the base framework for the bottom half of your design is finished, move on to the bust.

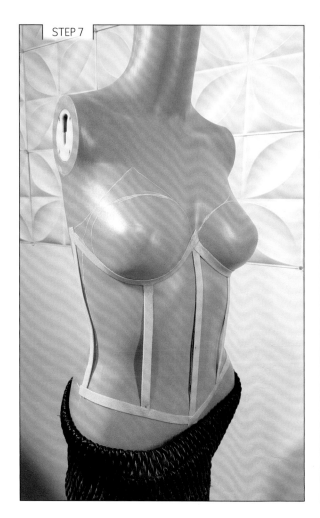

STEP 7

STEP 8

9 | Continue adding more Thibra strips to connect the framework of your design with intersecting interior lines. These strips will help add stability to the corset. A gridline was chosen for this demo, but you can connect these interior lines in the creative pattern of your choosing.

10 | Add an additional layer of Thibra strips to all of the outer framework pieces to increase stability by sandwiching the interior strips. For reference, your outer lines should have 2 layers while your interior lines have a single layer.

/ Note / *Additional layers can be applied for added stability or decoration.*

STEP 9

STEP 10

Completed Thibra Tex corset base

11 | Once your corset is complete, you can add D-ring straps to the back. Heat 1″ Thibra Tex strips, and wrap them around the flat side of each D-ring.

12 | One at a time, reheat each Thibra D-ring strip and press it into the back of your corset. Once all the pieces are attached, sandwich the rings with another long strip of Thibra.

/ Note / *Thibra Fine flowers can be added to complete the look. The tutorial for these flowers can be found on page 67.*

STEP 11

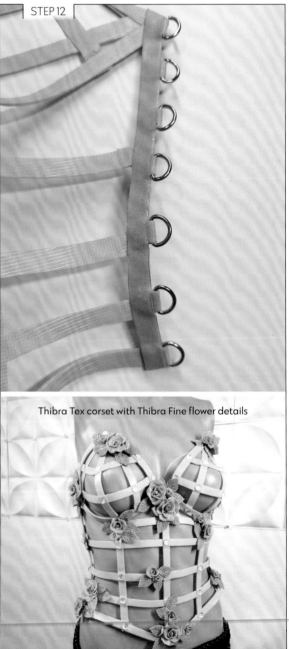

STEP 12

Thibra Tex corset with Thibra Fine flower details

THIBRA DEMO 2
CREATING ORGANIC SHAPES

SEE MORE INFORMATION *about Alkali on page 61.*

● by Alkali ●

This demonstration will showcase how to use Thibra Fine to sculpt small details for organic shapes. The sculpting techniques in this demo can be applied to any organic shape. Hand-sculpted accents add a unique and custom look to any cosplay creation.

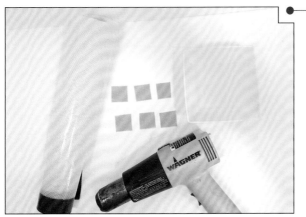

TOOLS AND MATERIALS

THIBRA FINE (PRECUT INTO 6 SQUARES OF 1″)

SILICONE MAT

HEAT GUN

SMALL BOWL OF COOL WATER

⚠ **SAFETY NOTE:** THERMOPLASTICS MAY BE VERY HOT TO THE TOUCH WHEN HEATED. USE PROTECTIVE GLOVES OR WAIT FOR THE MATERIAL TO COOL DOWN BEFORE HANDLING.

Instructions

1 | With your heat gun on a low setting, heat 1 of your 6 Thibra squares over your silicone mat. Thibra's melt point is 130°F/54.4°C, so your piece should become malleable after 10 seconds or so.

2 | Roll the heated Thibra into a small ball on your silicone mat.

/ Note / *Thibra will stick to most non-silicone surfaces.*

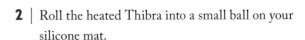

STEP 1

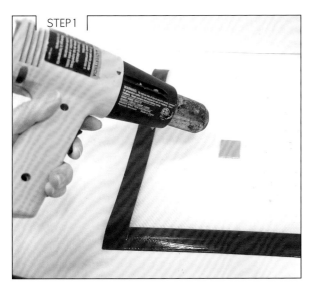

STEP 2

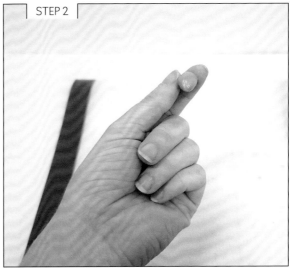

3 | With your thumb and index finger, press the Thibra into a flat oval shape over your silicone mat. Use even pressure to ensure the same thickness throughout; you don't want your piece to be too thin.

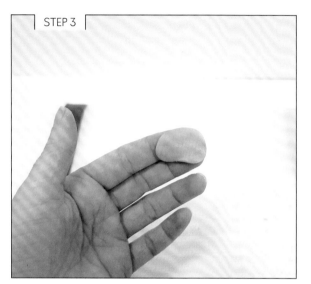

4 | Gently roll your Thibra oval to create a tiny rosebud.

/Tip/ Dip your fingers into your small bowl of water before rolling to help prevent fingerprints from transferring to the Thibra.

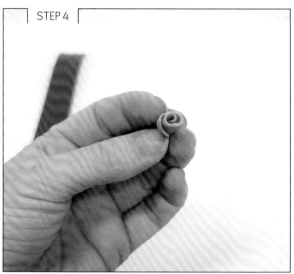

5 | Repeat Steps 1–2 with your remaining Thibra squares. Use your fingers to shape each piece into a small but thick petal shape.

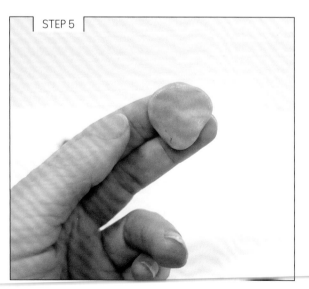

6 | Take your first petal, and reheat it until it's warm to the touch before wrapping it around your rosebud.

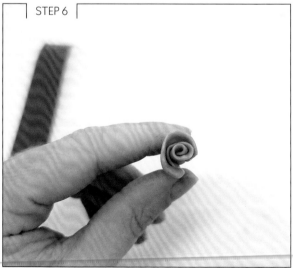

7 | Reheat the next petal with your heat gun, and apply it around the rosebud.

8 | Reheat your next petal, and use your fingers to shape it into a larger and thinner petal.

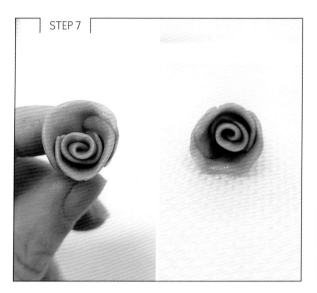

STEP 7

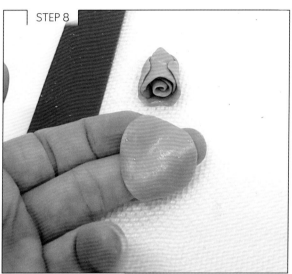

STEP 8

9 | With this petal still warm, wrap it around your rosebud base. Pull the edges of the petal away from the center to create an elegant blooming effect before adding ripples to give it a more organic look.

10 | With your remaining petals, use your fingers to shape these even thinner than the previous (bordering on see-through) to create a more realistic appearance.

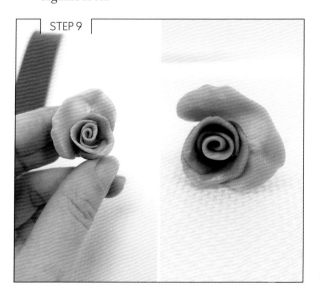

STEP 9

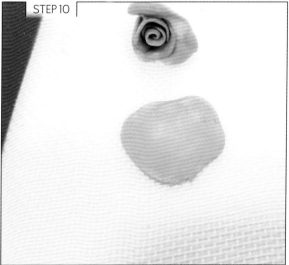

STEP 10

11 | Wrap the remaining petals around your rosebud base. Continue adding ripples and texture to these outer petals to complete your organic Thibra Fine rose.

STEP 11

Completed Thibra Fine rose

/ Thibra Tip / *You can heat up the back of your Thibra flower and press it gently to adhere it to a wide variety of surfaces.*

Completed Thibra Fine rose collection with sculpted leaves

Thibra rose collection applied to breastplate

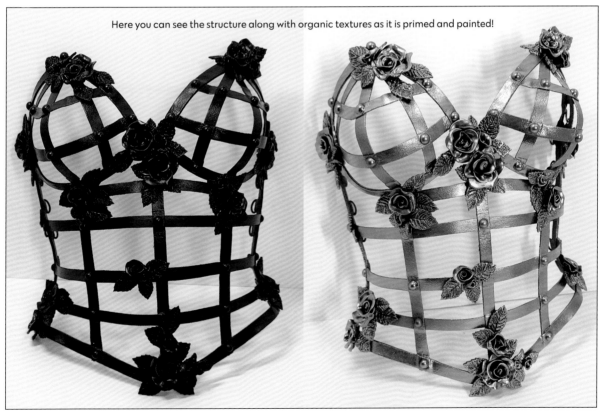

Here you can see the structure along with organic textures as it is primed and painted!

Varaform

What Is Varaform

Varaform is a lightweight thermoplastic material made from a cotton mesh that has been embedded in a thermoplastic resin; it activates at around 160°F. Originally developed as a medical cast alternative, it is nontoxic and skin safe, which makes it a handy material for those who have limited or cramped workspaces. As it is a mesh, it is very breathable and is a great choice for making large costume elements like mascot heads that can often cause overheating.

Using Varaform

Varaform can be heated with a heat gun or dipped in very hot water to reach its melting point.

Varaform is incredibly sticky, which is helpful when layering pieces, but it will stick to your work surface if it's not lined with wax paper or a silicone mat. Using silicone-tipped sculpting tools can be helpful.

/ Tip / *Keep a bowl of water handy, and dip your fingers in the water to keep the Varaform from sticking to your skin as you work!*

Try working in small areas and layering pieces together instead of making the whole element from a single cut of Varaform (unless you won't be covering the structure in another material later). Layers can be built up to add rigidity to the piece.

Varaform can be free-sculpted with care but often will be most successfully shaped over an existing positive mold or some interior structure. After heating, you have approximately 3 minutes of work time before you need to reheat the Varaform. The material can be folded and stretched as necessary to achieve the desired shape. It's helpful to use push pins to hold the Varaform in place on your positive mold as you're working and reheating other areas.

Uses

Varaform primarily has been used to make large animal and mascot heads in the past as it is breathable, durable, and lightweight. In cosplay, it could be useful as a base for oversized wigs, a wing structure, or other structural costume elements like eighteenth-century panniers or shoulder wings. Varaform can be used to modify shoes and other costume elements as a lighter alternative to other thermoplastics.

Finishing

Varaform can be left uncovered and painted with all kinds of paints. It also can be used as a base for other thermoplastics that require a base to retain their shape or as a structure for fabric coverings. The mesh finish allows elements such as feathers and yarn to be easily hand sewn onto or tied into the Varaform structure.

/ Note / *Keep in mind that similar to Worbla and other thermoplastics, Varaform may soften if left in a hot car or another high-temperature area!*

Paisley and Glue

Based in Chicago, Paisley and Glue has education in theatrical costume design, 20 years of sewing experience, and more than 10 years of professional experience making costumes for theater. She has been cosplaying for 7 years and has become highly involved in the Chicago cosplay community, attending various conventions, meetups, and charity events over the years. She enjoys instructing as well as learning from other members of the crafting and cosplay community, in addition to collaborating with other makers on various projects.

Costume ▶ Loki
(Original Regency
Variant) from *Loki*

*Photos by Brett Downen—
Downen Photography*

Paisley and Glue,
COSPLAYER

Costume ▶ Laudna from
Critical Role

Photo by Brett Downen—
Downen Photography

MAKING A CUSTOM FACE MASK

by Paisley and Glue

TOOLS AND MATERIALS

LIFE CAST OR OTHER HEAD FORM

ALUMINUM FOIL OR OTHER MATERIAL
AS A RELEASE AGENT

HEAT GUN OR BOILING WATER

VARAFORM

BOWL OF WATER

A good beginner project with Varaform is to make a mask based on your face cast. You can use a wig head in a pinch, but keep in mind that a heat gun will melt the Styrofoam. This example uses a positive face cast in Hydrocal.

Instructions

1 | Cover the head form in aluminum foil or another release agent. In this example, aluminum foil with a thin layer of Vaseline was used.

2 | Carefully heat the Varaform with a heat gun or in a pot of boiling water. The Varaform will get slightly shiny when it is ready to be worked.

3 | When the Varaform is ready to be handled, carefully drape it over the head shape, and start working it into the negative spaces, starting with the nose and eye sockets. Fold, clip, and stretch the Varaform as needed. Hold the Varaform in place as it starts to cool so it retains the desired shape.

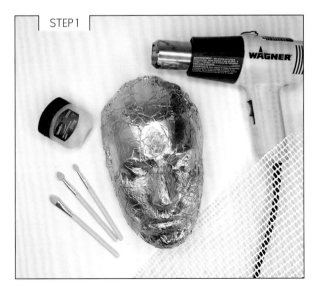

STEP 1

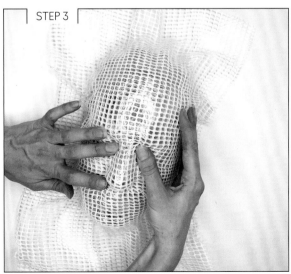

STEP 3

4 | If the Varaform cools off before you are finished, use the heat gun to reheat the plastic. Try not to reheat areas that have already been finished as the Varaform tends to flatten out again.

5 | When you are finished casting your head form, wait for the Varaform to cool completely before removing it (up to 30 minutes for thicker areas). Carefully peel the Varaform from the head form.

/ Note on Release Agents / If you used foil, it will likely stick to the Varaform and need to be peeled away from the mesh. If you used Vaseline, make sure to wash the Varaform in cold water to remove as much residue as possible before painting.

6 | Trim the mask if desired, leaving a small seam allowance. Place the mask back on the head form, and use the heat gun in those areas to fold back the seam allowance so the edges aren't sharp.

STEP 6

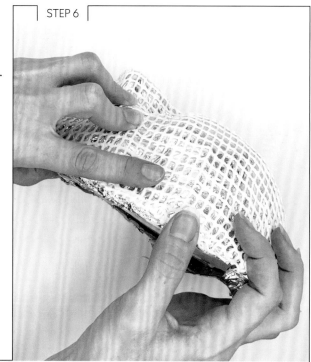

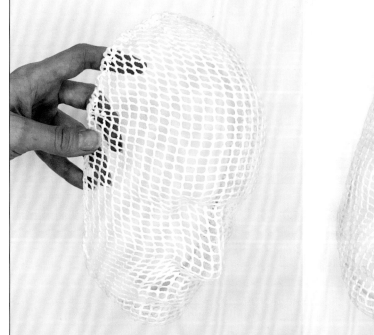

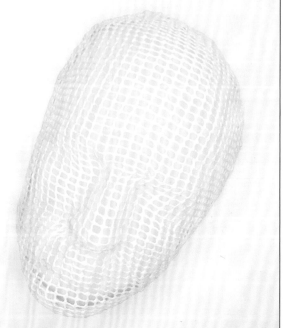

7 | Add embellishments, paints, and other decor to finish the mask.

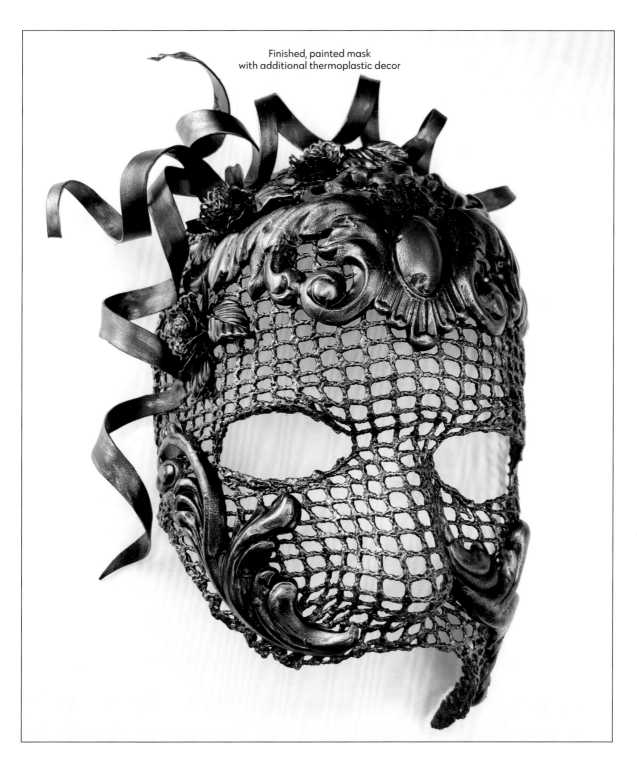

Finished, painted mask
with additional thermoplastic decor

Fosshape

What Is Fosshape?

Fosshape (pronounced *fozz–shape*) is a versatile thermoplastic distributed by Wonderflex World that begins as a soft felt that can be shrunk with steam to become a lightweight, semirigid plastic shell. Fosshape can be dyed; painted; or covered with fabric, foam, or other thermoplastics, making it a versatile choice for a build.

Uses

Fosshape can be used as a base for pieces like hats, large headdresses, and other small costume and prop pieces. It also can be used as a structural element within larger pieces, giving lightweight stability to gravity-defying costume elements. Sewing wire or boning to Fosshape gives extra rigidity to pieces.

Shrinking *Fosshape will shrink between 15% and 30%, depending on the rigidity desired. Keep this in mind when cutting out patterns. It's good practice to add some allowance for shrinkage to all edges (especially the outside edges, which can be trimmed away afterward).*

Keep in mind that using steam alone will stiffen the material into a more rigid felt but will allow for some flexibility. Pressure from a heat source like a steamer or iron will compress and harden the Fosshape much more.

Methods of Construction

- Steamed directly over a positive shape (optional: prestitching shaping seams)

- Steamed into flat, semirigid sheets, then cut out into pattern pieces and sewn together

Fosshape Options

There are several types of Fosshape on the market.

Fosshape 300: thinnest (white color)

Fosshape 400: medium (black color)

Fosshape 600: thickest (white color)

Layering Fosshape *Fosshape can be layered and fused using the pressure from a hand steamer or iron to build up the piece and add strength. It's sometimes beneficial to use this technique over stitched seams where the piece would otherwise have a weaker spot.*

Things to Consider

Similar to other thermoplastics, Fosshape can lose its shape slightly over time and is susceptible to creasing and crushing; however, it isn't easily torn. Using wire around the edges of the piece and/or stuffing the negative space inside can help mitigate crushing to a certain extent, but using Fosshape to support large areas with no other structure can cause a piece to break down over time.

Fosshape base with additional boning structure for Marvel's Thor-inspired cloak

Becoming Thor,
COSPLAYER

Costume **Thor Odinson from *Thor***
Photo by Afrodyte Charlotte Photography

Fosshape is more lightweight than most other thermoplastics and also can be more comfortable against the skin as it retains a softer, more breathable finish than other thermoplastics, even after being steamed into shape.

Fosshape can be dyed, but pastel colors will be the most successful (on white Fosshape), and dye meant for polyester must be used.

⚠ **SAFETY NOTE:** FOSSHAPE IS NONTOXIC AS IT IS HEATED, WHICH MAKES IT A GREAT CHOICE FOR INDOOR USE. IT NEEDS ONLY A HANDHELD STEAMER TO BE ACTIVATED; CARE SHOULD BE EXERCISED WHEN USING A STEAMER AS THE STEAM CAN EASILY BURN SKIN. THE TEMPERATURE REQUIRED IS ABOUT 200°F.

A HEAT GUN OR IRON ALSO CAN BE USED TO SHRINK AND STIFFEN FOSSHAPE (ESPECIALLY THE PRESSURE FROM AN IRON) BUT CAN EASILY SCORCH OR BURN A HOLE IN THE FOSSHAPE.

Marvel's Thor-inspired cloak worn by cosplayer Becoming Thor, costume by Paisley and Glue.

Fosshape structural shoulder base

Paisley and Glue,
COSPLAYER

Costume   Maleficent from
Disney's *Maleficent*

Photo by Alexandra Lee Studios

Photo by Maggie Hofmann

Maleficent cosplay featuring
shoulders built out with Fosshape
by Paisley and Glue

SEE MORE INFORMATION
about Paisley and Glue on page 73.

FOSSHAPE DEMO 1
MAKING A FOSSHAPE SKULLCAP

by Paisley and Glue

TOOLS AND MATERIALS

FOSSHAPE WEIGHT OF YOUR CHOICE

HEAD FORM (PADDED OUT WITH FELT TO YOUR DESIRED SIZE/SHAPE)

SKULLCAP PATTERN

HANDHELD STEAMER, STEAM IRON, OR HEAT GUN

WIRE (OPTIONAL)

½ YARD NARROW ELASTIC

PUSHPINS

A good beginner project with Fosshape is to make a skullcap to use as a base for a larger hat, wig, or headdress or even just to bulk out a Styrofoam wig head to make it closer to your actual head size!

/Note/ While it is possible to form the Fosshape over a head shape with no seams, you will likely get some wrinkling at the edges. The most successful way to get a very rounded shape, like a head, will be to sew some seams into the Fosshape before heat shrinking it down.

Instructions

1 | Cut out the skullcap pattern, and trace the pieces onto the Fosshape felt.

2 | Cut out the pattern pieces, leaving an extra ¼″ of seam allowance on seam edges and 3″ on outer edges to allow for shrinkage. Stitch the seams together with a short stitch or zigzag on a new stitch line, and trim down seam allowance to reduce bulk.

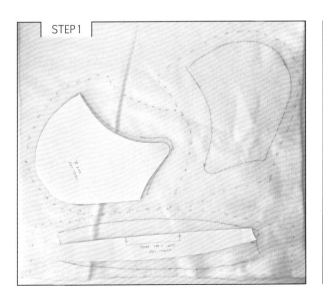

STEP 1

STEP 2

3 | Pull the Fosshape over the head form, and pin the elastic around the hairline to keep it loosely in place. This is to ensure that the Fosshape does not distort as you steam as well as to distribute any fullness to avoid creases.

4 | Using the hand steamer about 3˝ from the Fosshape, begin at the crown of the head, and slowly move the steam down across the head in long strokes, overlapping each stroke slightly so the Fosshape shrinks evenly. As you steam, it may be necessary to stop and move your elastic down slightly as the Fosshape shrinks to avoid forming holes.

5 | After you finish one pass around the head, you can make additional passes with the steamer held closer to the surface of the Fosshape. You can even use the steamer or iron to apply pressure to the Fosshape to shrink and stiffen it as much as possible.

6 | After the Fosshape has cooled, it can be pulled from the head. However, keep in mind that a form with an undercut may need to be split at the center back and stitched back together with a zigzag stitch.

7 | Cut the Fosshape skullcap to the desired shape. Millinery wire can be sewn to the edge of the skullcap with a machine zigzag stitch or hand blanket stitch for extra strength. If the cap gets warped or squished with handling, you can apply steam again to reshape it.

The skullcap can now be incorporated into your project!

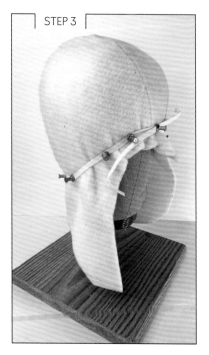
STEP 3

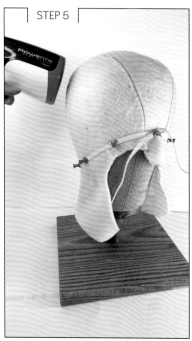
STEP 5

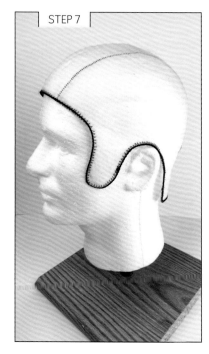
STEP 7

MAKING ANIMAL EARS

by Paisley and Glue

SEE MORE INFORMATION *about Paisley and Glue on page 73.*

TOOLS AND MATERIALS

FOSSHAPE (ANY TYPE)

HANDHELD STEAMER, STEAM IRON, OR HEAT GUN

ANIMAL EAR PATTERN (OF YOUR CHOOSING)

MILLINER WIRE

PAINTS OR DYE

FAUX FUR

HOT GLUE GUN OR NEEDLE AND THREAD

Fosshape is a great material to use for structuring animal ears. This demo is one example, but it can be used to make a variety of styles.

/ Note / *To make the animal ears in this example, the Fosshape was steamed into flat pieces, then cut out with a pattern and assembled.*

Instructions

1 | Using a hand steamer or steam iron, shrink and flatten the Fosshape until you have enough treated surface area to cut out your ear patterns.

2 | Trace your ear pattern, and cut out the shapes, leaving seam allowance at the base of the ear to stitch to a hat or wig later. If your ear has any seams, use a sewing machine to stitch them together by butting the edges with a zigzag stitch.

3 | Optional: Use the zigzag stitch on your sewing machine to sew wire to the edge of the ear for rigidity and posing options later. A 19-gauge millinery wire is used for this example.

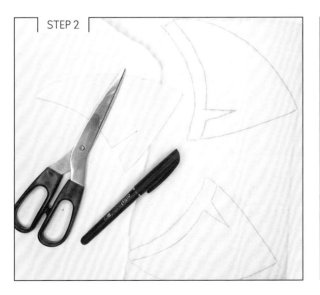

STEP 2

STEP 3

4 | With your paint or dye, use a dry brush technique or an airbrush to paint the inside of the ear. Typically this is the part where an animal has no fur.

5 | Trace the ear pattern onto the faux fur, adding a ½″ seam allowance, and carefully cut it out using a razor blade to cut only the fabric backing (this cutting method will preclude damaging any of the fur). Sew the dart, if present, and trim the seam allowance.

STEP 4

STEP 5

6 | Use your hot glue gun or needle and thread to carefully roll ¼″ of the seam allowance over to hide the cut edge.

7 | Stitch or glue the faux fur to the back of the ear, wrapping the edge of the fur around the edge of the ear to hide the wire and edge of the Fosshape. Glue or stitch the edge of the fur to the ear.

STEP 6

STEP 7

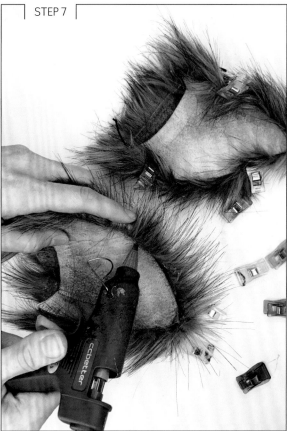

8 | Using the seam allowance of the ear, stitch or glue the ear to your hat, wig, or headband. Once finished, trim any stray fur fiber.

/Tip/ *Another way to hide your seam allowance is by cutting holes into your hat for the ears to slide into!*

STEP 8

Finished ears ready to be attached to a hat, wig, or headband

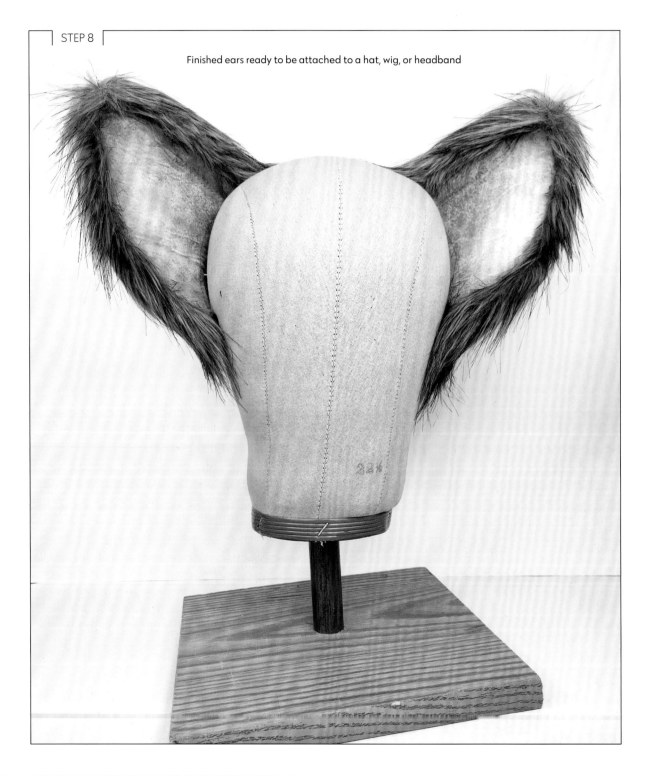

Insulation XPS Foam

What Is Insulation XPS Foam?

Also known as Foamular, XPS foam is an extremely lightweight and rigid material. XPS is styrene plastic that is foamed before the extrusion process. XPS foam is most commonly used as wall insulation in homes, but its uses are widespread.

Uses

XPS foam can be used as the foundation for many large-scale prop pieces. It offers superior rigidity while remaining lightweight. With its ability to be carved into shape, many cosplayers add much of their fine detail directly onto the surface. When covered with the right thermoplastic, creating a composite, it creates an extremely lightweight and durable prop.

Methods of Construction

XPS foam is a universal material that can be formed both manually and via machine. It can easily be carved with most sharp tools, for example, a utility knife. Rotary tools such as Dremel tools and sanding drums may be used to smooth out surfaces and hard edges.

Since XPS foam is a styrene-based material, it can be cut safely by a laser cutter. Due to its excellent machinability, it can be carved directly using a CNC router to replicate highly accurate detailing from 3D models.

Insulation XPS Foam Options

There are several types of insulation foam on the market.

Most common compressive strength:
15psi and 25psi

Thicknesses: from ½″ to 3″ thick in ½″ increments

Colors: pink, blue, green

Things to Consider

For cosplay, XPS foam can be carved but not heat formed. XPS foam is sensitive to many chemical solvents, requiring the user to seal the foam with a product such as Epsilon or to wrap it in a material such as EVA foam or Worbla. It can be cut/carved with a box cutter or hot wire cut and sanded to shape with a sanding drum. Hot glue should be used to glue pieces together. Using contact cement or a heat gun directly on the surface will melt the insulation foam.

⚠ **SAFETY NOTE:** WHEN CARVING OR SANDING XPS FOAM, IT IS IMPORTANT TO HAVE ADEQUATE EYE AND BREATHING PROTECTION. WEAR GLOVES WHEN TOUCHING THIS PRODUCT AS IT MAY IRRITATE THE SKIN, AND WEAR A RESPIRATOR WHEN USING A HOT WIRE CUTTER TO CUT IT. SHAPING XPS FOAM CAN CREATE A LOT OF FINE PARTICULATE DURING ABRASIVE PROCESSES. XPS FOAM IS VERY SUSCEPTIBLE TO CERTAIN CHEMICALS IN COMMON PAINTS AND ADHESIVES, SO BE AWARE OF ANYTHING WITH SOLVENTS THAT COULD MELT THE FOAM.

WRAPPING XPS FOAM WITH WORBLA

by Tiffany Gordon Cosplay

SEE MORE INFORMATION *about Tiffany Gordon Cosplay on page 11.*

Make a set of dual blades from the popular Capcom® game *Monster Hunter* that can break apart into two pieces for easy transportation. This technique can be used for many types of prop weapons.

/ Note / *This demo is broken into three sections.*

PART 1
INNER STRUCTURE WITH CPVC PIPES

TOOLS AND MATERIALS

CPVC PIPE

PROP WEAPON PATTERN

SAW

MALE AND FEMALE CPVC SLIP STAINLESS STEEL ADAPTERS

LOW-GRIT SANDPAPER (RECOMMENDED 60–120)

TWO-PART EPOXY

SAFETY GLASSES

DISPOSABLE GLOVES

Instructions

1 | We want this prop to disassemble where the blade meets the handle. To do this, cut 2 measured pieces of CPVC pipe with your saw, one sized for the handle and one for the blade. These pieces are for the inner structure of one of the dual blades.

/ Tip / *If you're also making dual weapon props, repeat all steps for your second prop.*

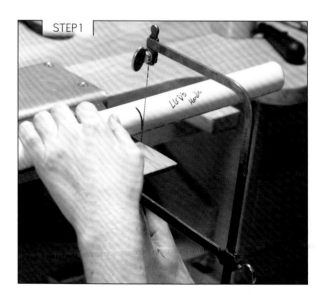
STEP 1

For the next step, you will need your male and female CPVC slip stainless steel adapters. These will allow you to remove the blade portion of your prop from the handle for storage or travel.

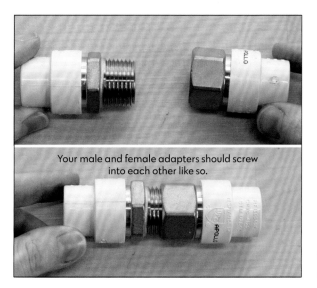

Your male and female adapters should screw into each other like so.

2 | Lay your pieces alongside your original pattern to ensure that your inner structure will fit within your prop.

/ Note / *If your CPVC pipes are too long, simply mark and saw off any additional length.*

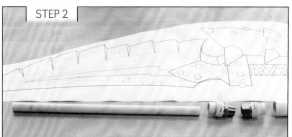

STEP 2

3 | Using your low-grit sandpaper, sand the ends of the CPVC pipe and the insides of both the male and the female adapters. This is so the epoxy will have a better surface texture to grab onto; if left smooth the glue could eventually fail.

4 | Adequately mix both epoxy parts together, and apply the glue around the tip of the first CPVC pipe before attaching one of the adapters. Wipe away any excess glue with a paper towel. Repeat this for the second CPVC pipe with the opposite adapter and then wait at least 24 hours for the epoxy to fully cure.

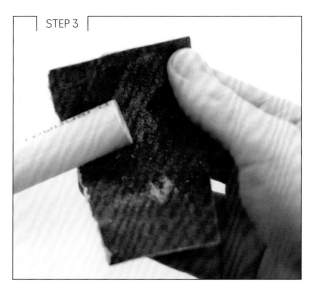

STEP 3

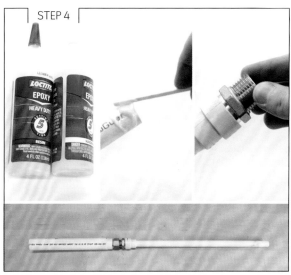

STEP 4

TOOLS AND MATERIALS

PROP WEAPON PATTERN

INSULATION XPS FOAM BOARD

COMPLETED CPVC PIPE INNER STRUCTURE

PERMANENT MARKER (LIKE A SHARPIE)

HOT GLUE GUN

WEIGHTS

BOX CUTTER OR HOT WIRE CUTTER

CUTTING MAT

HEAT-RESISTANT GLOVES

SAFETY GLASSES

DUST MASK OR RESPIRATOR

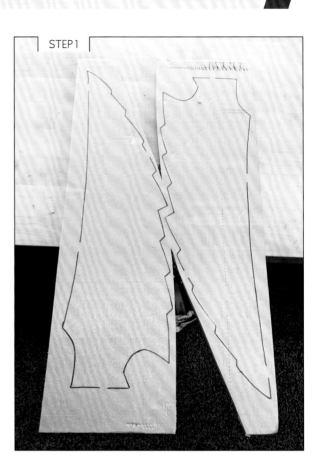

STEP 1

Instructions

1 | Cut out your paper prop weapon pattern, and place it over your insulation foam. Using a black Sharpie marker, trace the outline of the blade three separate times. You will need 3 pieces for each prop weapon.

2 | Cut out all your blade pieces on your cutting mat with a box cutter or with a hot wire cutter for more intricate designs.

3 | Take one of your three blade pieces, and place your inner CPVC structure on top where it will fit best inside your prop. Trace the outline of the CPVC using your Sharpie marker.

4 | Cut out this section with a box cutter over your cutting mat until it can be completely removed.

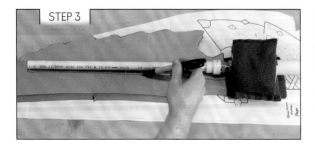

STEP 3

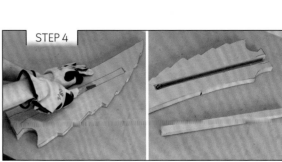

STEP 4

5 | Place your CPVC pipe structure into the section you just removed, and place your weights over the insulation foam to hold it in place. Using your hot glue gun, apply glue down the edges of the pipe where it touches the foam before going down the length once again with a zigzag motion. This pattern will ensure all the pieces fuse together. Wait for the hot glue to dry completely, and repeat this step for the opposite side.

6 | Now it's time to glue the additional blade cutouts to the center piece. Keep in mind you will need to work fast for this step, so have everything set out and ready before you start applying hot glue. Take your first blade piece, and quickly apply a moderate amount of hot glue to one side. While the glue is still hot, place it on top of the center CPVC pipe piece. Hold firmly in place until the glue is dry. Repeat with the opposite blade piece.

/ Tip / *You don't need to cover the entire blade surface with glue—just enough for it all to stick together!*

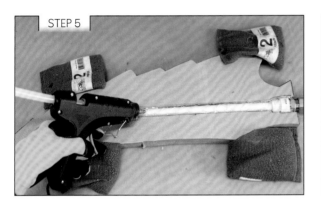
STEP 5

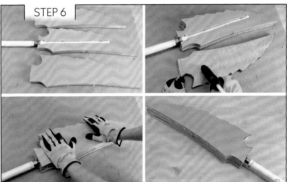
STEP 6

7 | You should now have a full blade piece and a handle that can unscrew into two pieces.

8 | At this point, you can start carving your blade into your desired shape.

/ Note / *You can use many tools to do this, but be sure to wear a dust mask or respirator for this step so you don't inhale any foam dust.*

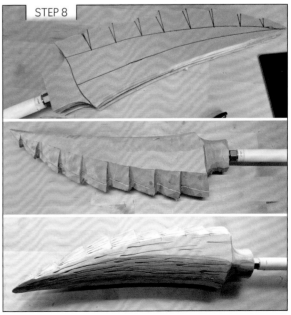
STEP 8

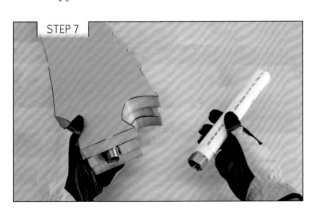
STEP 7

TOOLS AND MATERIALS

COMPLETED INSULATION FOAM BLADE

WORBLA'S BLACK ART

HEAT GUN

HEAT-RESISTANT GLOVES

SCISSORS

CLAY-WORKING TOOLS

/ Note / *Worbla's Black Art is similar to Worbla's Finest Art but has a smoother texture. It is less adhesive but allows for more details and sculpting.*

Instructions

1 | Place your completed foam blade on top of the Worbla, and cut out 2 pieces large enough to encapsulate the entire blade.

STEP 1

2 | Heat your first piece of Worbla with a heat gun until it starts to become flexible.

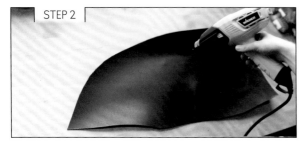

STEP 2

3 | With your sheet of Worbla still hot and flexible, place it over your insulation foam blade.

STEP 3

4 | Apply heat to the Worbla again until it starts to drape over the top portion of your blade. Evenly distribute the heat as you work so that the Worbla maintains an even temperature.

/ Note / *Be sure to apply heat to the Worbla carefully and never apply it directly to the insulation foam. Direct heat will cause the foam to melt.*

STEP 4

5 | Now that the Worbla is draped over your blade, you can focus on individual sections. Heat smaller sections with your heat gun before using your fingers to press the Worbla into any curves.

/Note/ *The Worbla can get hot, so wear your heat-resistant gloves if you're sensitive to heat. For the finer details, heat the Worbla once again, and go in with your clay-sculpting tools.*

6 | Leaving about an inch around the entire piece, cut off any excess Worbla.

/Tip/ *It's easier to cut Worbla when it's slightly hot. So if you're having trouble, hit it with your heat gun.*

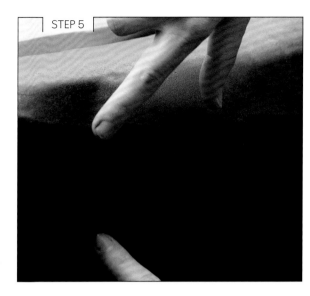

STEP 5

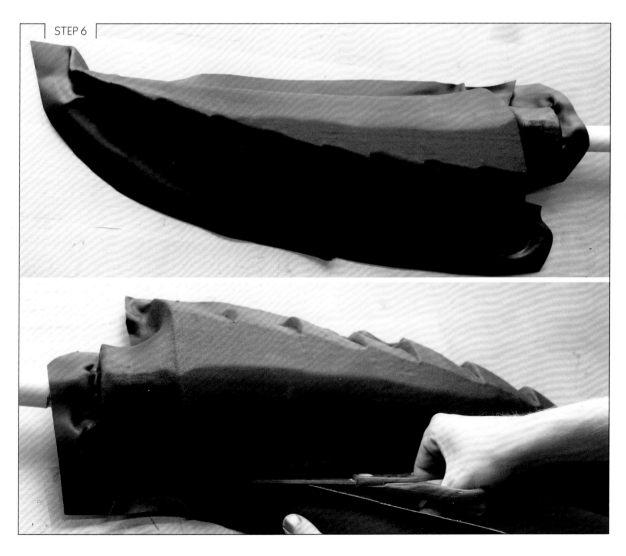

STEP 6

7 | Repeat Steps 2–3 for the other side of your blade.

/ Tip / *To ensure a good bond between both of your Worbla pieces, be sure to also heat the connecting points of your first Worbla piece when connecting.*

8 | Repeat Steps 4–6 with your second Worbla piece.

9 | Carefully cut the seam closer to the edge of your blade, applying heat as needed as you cut away the excess Worbla.

STEP 9

10 | Starting with your fingers, smooth out the seam while the Worbla is still flexible before going in with a flat-surface clay tool.

11 | Now that the foam is completely covered in Worbla, you can go in with your clay tools to add more details to the blade.

12 | Once you're finished with your blade details, you can add foam elements to finish your dual blade or prop weapon!

STEP 11

STEP 12

Mulholland Art

Mulholland Art is a brilliant maker from Philadelphia, Pennsylvania, who is known for his incredibly detailed costumes, props, and character replicas. "I learned intuitively at a young age that creating was a kind of act of rebellion against a state of unbeing. From my formal training in art school to my studies of language, my life has largely been about discovering and sharing ways to create. Cosplay is a unique intersection of culture and art that demonstrates a common reverence for finely crafted things and their creators, which is why it has been my focus for the last seven years. I believe that revelry for creative endeavors is our greatest saving grace."

A

B

C

Costume ▶ Kulve Taroth Alpha Armor Set from *Monster Hunter: World*

A–B: Photo by Knorr Designs—Jarred Knorr

C: Photo by World of Gwendana—Kyle Williams

Mulholland Art.

COSPLAYER

Costume ▶ Rajang Armor Set from *Monster Hunter World: Iceborne*

Photo by Knorr Designs—Jarred Knorr

LARGE-SCALE SCULPTING

• by Mulholland Art •

TOOLS AND MATERIALS

PROP OR WEAPON PATTERN

INSULATION XPS FOAM BOARD

PERMANENT MARKER (LIKE A SHARPIE)

HOT GLUE GUN

WEIGHTS

BOX CUTTER OR HOT WIRE CUTTER

CUTTING MAT

DUST MASK OR RESPIRATOR

This palamute stands about 4´ tall at the shoulders and was made with 2˝ foam sheets, so each square represents 2˝.

The most complicated part of one of these projects is the planning. Choose your foam considering the following: Thicker foam sheets will require less planning but more carving, and thinner foam sheets will require more planning but less carving. Consider which suits you better. Use grid paper, and match one unit on the grid to the thickness of your foam. So when using 2˝ foam, each square will represent 2˝. Using a profile view of the sculpture will eliminate the need to plan both halves if it is symmetrical. Using a frontal view will require a layer for the entire sculpture unless the object is symmetrical from front to back.

Instructions

1 | Draw the project in profile view on the grid paper with the proportions that it will ultimately have, bearing in mind the length each unit represents.

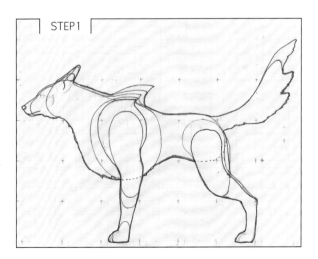

STEP 1

2 | Draw the front, rear, top, and bottom drawings from the profile drawing.

It's very important to maintain consistency across all the drawings for the location of the parts. Once all of the drawings have been generated, locate and transfer the upper, lower, front, and back limits of each layer to the profile drawing. Starting with the center layer and moving outward to the side layers usually works best. Bear in mind that the center layers often will not contain features like ears or arms, while outer layers will not have features like tails. For those situations, a broken line can be used for a layer that is smaller than a sequential layer, such as is the case for the palamute's ears, arms, and legs.

3 | Scale up the profile drawing using large grid paper if it's available. Any large-scale paper will work, but grid paper is ideal.

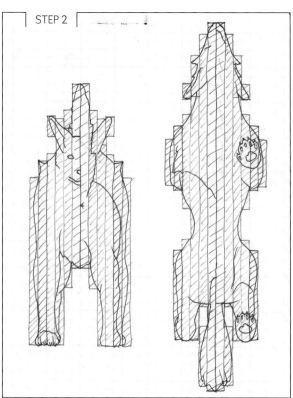

STEP 2

4 | Transfer each layer to the foam. It's very important to create some way of registering subsequent layers and to color-code to avoid confusion. Start with your largest layer, and add any marks or lines that will help line up the connecting layers as you're cutting. This will help as you begin to assemble all layers of XPS foam moving forward.

| Tip | Many types of glue work well enough, but ideally you will use a glue that has a medium-thick body and dries to be semiflexible. A hot glue gun will work very well with this. Very stiff glues will dull razor blades very quickly, and gummy glues will gunk them up. Do not use silicone adhesives, epoxies, Super Glue, or construction adhesives. Many types of glue contain aggressive solvents that can melt your foam. If you are unsure, test your glue on a piece of scrap in a well-ventilated area.

5 | Glue all the foam layers together. Once your piece is fully assembled, it's ready to be carved. At this stage, it's just a matter of getting a smooth transition between all of the layers. There is almost always more material present than it appears, so it's fine to be aggressive and lop big chunks off at this stage.

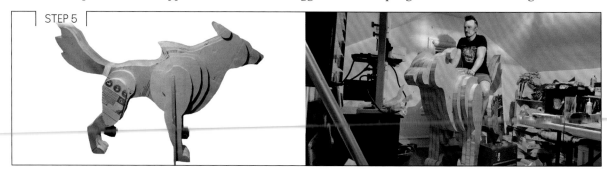

STEP 5

6 | Continue to smooth the transitions between layers and work to keep the project symmetrical. Using a marker helps to prevent getting lost.

7 | Once the layers are smoothed together, it's time to lay out some of the larger details, like musculature.

8 | Carving the musculature in an exaggerated way is advisable for any sculpture that is going to have fur or feathers carved later. For scales and smooth surfaces, a more modest approach might be appropriate.

STEP 6

STEP 8

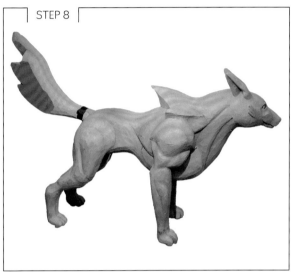

9 | Carving details like fur or scales can be tedious. Take breaks, listen to your favorite podcasts, and just chip away at it.

STEP 9

10 Seal the insulation foam sculpture before painting, with Mod Podge, FlexBond, or even wood glue.

/Tips/

• *It's worth noting that bubbles may appear under FlexBond due to changes in humidity or off-gassing from paints/glues.*

• *Seal with Mod Podge or wood glue before or after FlexBond. The benefit of FlexBond is that it will make the sculpture much more resistant to breaking as it is not as brittle as Mod Podge or wood glue. The combination of Mod Podge and FlexBond gives a nonbrittle strength that neither provides on its own.*

• *Other things one might consider sealing with are urethane resins, aqua resin, epoxy putty, Worbla, and even latex or urethane rubbers.*

• *Virtually all spray paints (including Plasti Dip) will dissolve the insulation foam if applied directly and therefore may only be used after sealing.*

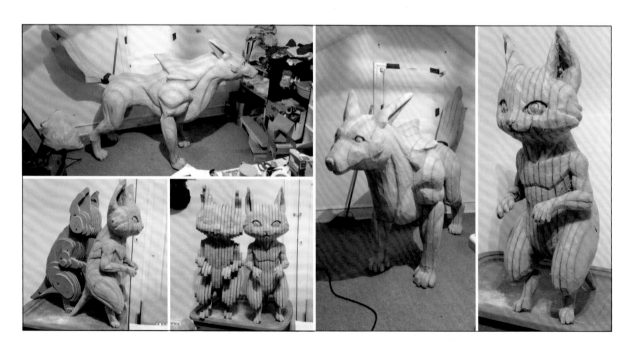

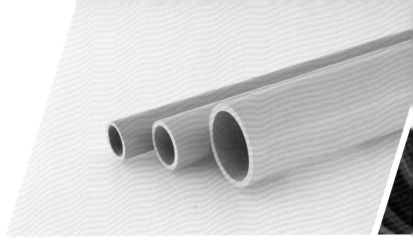

PVC Pipe

What Is PVC?

PVC (or polyvinyl chloride) is a common replacement for metal piping in the plumbing industry. It is a popular choice for plastics because of its strength, durability, easy installation, and low cost.

Uses

PVC pipes are powerful tools for creating a strong framework for the internal structures of costumes and props. Straight sections are often used in the core of long props such as swords, scythes, and staffs. Many larger-than-life cosplayers build entire cages to frame out suits of armor, vehicles, and even wings! Since PVC piping offers a standardized system of construction, many cosplayers design their large costumes to be modular, with the ability to be easily disassembled for transportation.

Methods of Construction

PVC pipe can be cut using hand saws, PVC cutters, and rotary cutting disks. Be sure to sand away any sharp edges after cutting. PVC can easily be bent when carefully heated to create smooth arcs and creative geometry. A wide variety of off-the-shelf angle connectors is available for creating strong joints.

PVC Options

There are two thickness standards for PVC piping:

- Schedule 40—thinner

- Schedule 80—thicker

PVC pipe is normally measured by its inner diameter measurement. It ranges from ⅛″ diameter to 12″ diameter, with lengths up to 10′ long!

Similarly, CPVC is a thermoplastic that is molded into many of the same products as PVC, and it tends to come in smaller diameters. It's considered much more flexible and can handle a higher temperature threshold.

Things to Consider

- It's very hard to achieve sharp bends with PVC pipe. For such shapes, you will need specific fittings such as elbow fittings.

- You should always heat PVC pipe slowly.

⚠ **SAFETY NOTE:** DO NOT BURN PVC PIPE! HEATING AND BURNING PVC PIPE CAN RELEASE TOXIC FUMES. YOU SHOULD ALWAYS WEAR A RESPIRATOR AND WORK IN A WELL-VENTILATED AREA.

SEE MORE INFORMATION *about Tiffany Gordon Cosplay on page 11.*

PVC PIPE DEMO 1

BENDING CPVC/PVC PIPE

● by Tiffany Gordon Cosplay ●

CPVC Pipes Versus PVC Pipes

• CPVC is yellowish in color, and PVC is white.

• Either can be found at hardware stores.

• CPVC can withstand temperatures up to 200°F, whereas PVC can withstand temperatures up to 140°F.

• CPVC is easier to bend than is PVC.

• PVC comes in a larger range of sizes.

• CPVC has more smaller attachment pieces for making parts disassemble.

• Either can be cut with a saw.

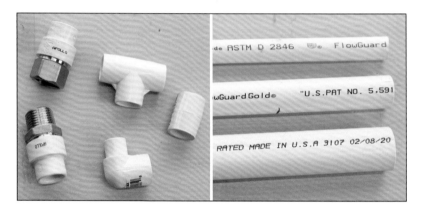

⚠ **SAFETY NOTE:** BOTH CPVC AND PVC PIPES RELEASE TOXIC FUMES WHEN HEATED. YOU SHOULD ALWAYS WEAR A RESPIRATOR, WORK IN A WELL-VENTILATED AREA OR OUTSIDE, AND MAKE SURE YOUR FURRY CRITTERS ARE NOT IN THE SAME ROOM WHEN HEATING THESE PIECES.

Using CPVC/PVC pipes as the inner structure for costumes and props is a great way to keep your projects lightweight. But what if your project has curves? Look no further as this demo will show you how to bend this versatile material to your advantage.

TOOLS AND MATERIALS

HEAT-RESISTANT GLOVES

HEAT-RESISTANT SURFACE

HEAT GUN

RESPIRATOR

CPVC OR PVC PIPE

PERMANENT MARKER (LIKE A SHARPIE)

Instructions

/ Note / *For this demo, CPVC pipe is being used.*

1 | Mark your CPVC or PVC pipe where you want it to bend. This will be your guide for where to apply heat.

2 | Heat the marked area with your heat gun, and slowly rotate the pipe so the heat distributes evenly.

/ Tip / *Avoid staying in one spot for too long. CPVC and PVC will burn when overheated.*

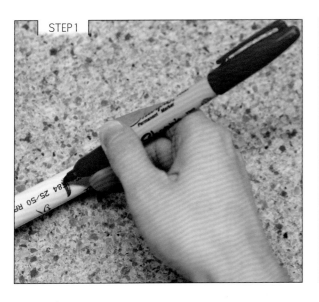
STEP 1

STEP 2

3 | When the marked area becomes malleable, turn off your heat gun, and bend the pipe to your desired angle.

4 | Hold the pipe at your desired angle until it cools. Once cool, it will be solid, and you can move on to any other areas that need bending by repeating these steps!

STEP 3

PVC Vinyl

What Is PVC Vinyl?

PVC Vinyl is a thick, transparent, fabric-like plastic typically used in health care, building and construction, and even fashion (for items such as clothing and bags).

Uses

While bulkier and heavier than heat transfer vinyl (HTV), or cellophanes, PVC Vinyl is more durable and still retains transparency for costume pieces like such as wings and billowing skirts.

It can be easily stretched over frames to create lightweight panels without the weight penalties of rigid plastics.

Methods of Construction

PVC Vinyl can easily be sewn as well as heated up and stretched over frames. It can be cut and trimmed with classic fabric tools such as scissors, shears, and knives.

PVC Vinyl Options

PVC Vinyl comes in almost any color imaginable in both opaque and transparent variants.

Things to Consider

• PVC Vinyl often comes folded, which results in creases. You can smooth out this imperfection easily with a heat gun.

• If overheated or overstretched, holes can form in your PVC Vinyl.

⚠ **SAFETY NOTE:** ALWAYS USE A RESPIRATOR WHILE USING A HEAT GUN ON PVC VINYL. SIMILARLY TO PVC PIPES, HEATING AND BURNING PVC VINYL CAN RELEASE TOXIC FUMES.

Plexi Cosplay

Plexi Cosplay of Baltimore, Maryland, started cosplaying in 2016 and creates her costumes from scratch. She is an award-winning artist whose goal is to continue competing and raising the bar for the cosplay community. Her work includes very detailed foam fabrication, SFX makeup, electronics, wig styling, sewing, and leatherwork. Plexi also educates and supports the cosplay community through tutorials, live workshops, contest judging, blogging, hosting panels, and more.

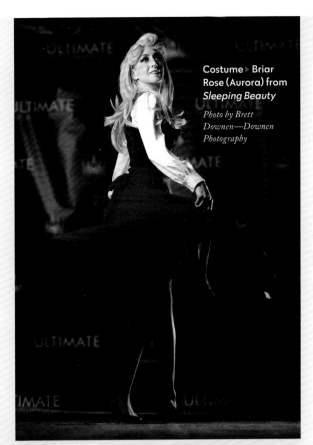

Costume ▶ Briar Rose (Aurora) from *Sleeping Beauty*

Photo by Brett Downen—Downen Photography

Photo by Kelly Heck Photography

Plexi Cosplay,
COSPLAYER

**Costume ▶ Original Magnamalo/
Nargacuga Armor Set from** *Monster
Hunter Rise*

*Photo by Brett Downen—Downen
Photography*

STRETCHING AND OVERLAYING PVC VINYL OVER A PVC STRUCTURE

by Plexi Cosplay

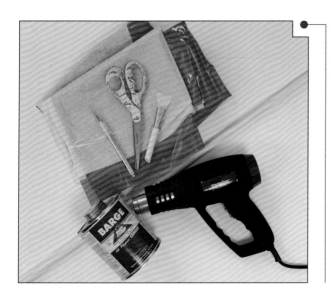

TOOLS AND MATERIALS

½″ PVC OR CPVC PIPE

PVC VINYL IN TWO COLORS:
BASE COLOR AND OVERLAY COLOR

CONTACT CEMENT

TACKY SPRAY GLUE

SCISSORS OR UTILITY KNIFE (X-ACTO)

HEAT GUN

PERMANENT MARKER (LIKE A SHARPIE)

BLACK PAINT

PAINTBRUSHES

RESPIRATOR

Instructions

1 | Use your heat gun on the high setting at the midpoint of your PVC pipe. After about 30 seconds, the pipe will soften and can be bent to your desired angle. For this project, I'm folding the pipe at an acute angle for a triangular panel.

⚠ **SAFETY NOTE:** PVC RELEASES TOXIC FUMES IF OVERHEATED, SO WORK IN A VENTILATED AREA AND WEAR A PROPER RESPIRATOR.

STEP 1

2 | To curve the "bones" of the framework, slowly move the heat gun up and down the shaft of the piping on high heat to soften the PVC. This takes patience, but with some force, the piping will eventually bend as the plastic warms and softens.

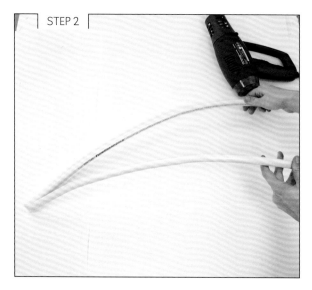

STEP 2

3 | Lay your base color of PVC Vinyl over the PVC framework. Cut the vinyl about 2˝ from the outside of the piping.

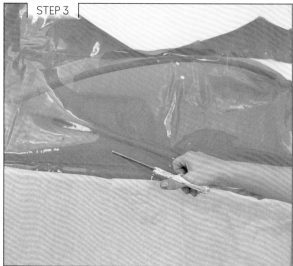

STEP 3

4 | Set your heat gun to the low setting, and gently warm the PVC Vinyl to smooth out any creases or bumps.

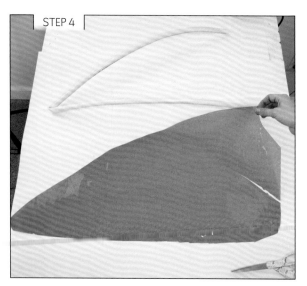

STEP 4

5 | Lay your PVC Vinyl gently on your pipe framework, and use a Sharpie to trace where the framework meets the vinyl. Remove the vinyl, and flip it so the right side is lying downward.

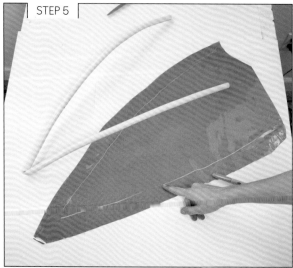

STEP 5

6 | Apply contact cement to the vinyl with a brush or spatula at the Sharpie line outward toward the edge. Apply contact cement to the entire PVC pipe framework. Allow it to dry.

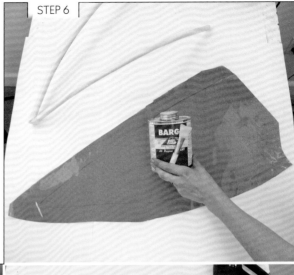

STEP 6

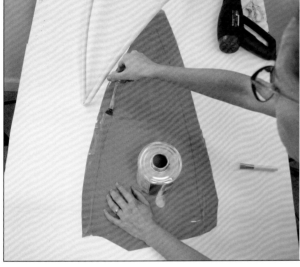

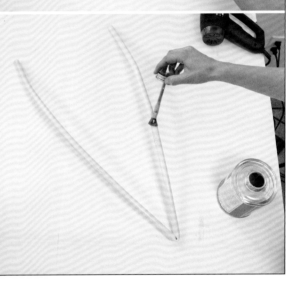

7 | Once the contact cement is dry, gently lay the PVC Vinyl on the framework, while lining up the Sharpie line with the frame underneath.

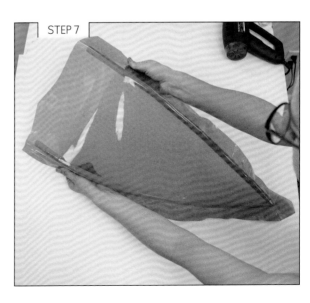

STEP 7

8 | Flip the piece right side down, and clip the curves of the vinyl on the outside edges. This will help the vinyl have smooth edges as it's folded onto the framework. Next, trim the edges of the vinyl to about 1½″ from the pipe for neatness.

9 | Gently pull the vinyl taut, and fold it around the framework. This will cause the contact cement to adhere.

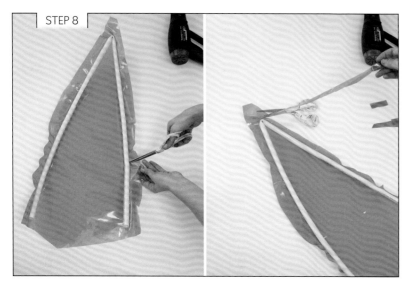

10 | Use your heat gun on the low setting to smooth out the vinyl once more, and press the vinyl onto the framework as it's pulled taut.

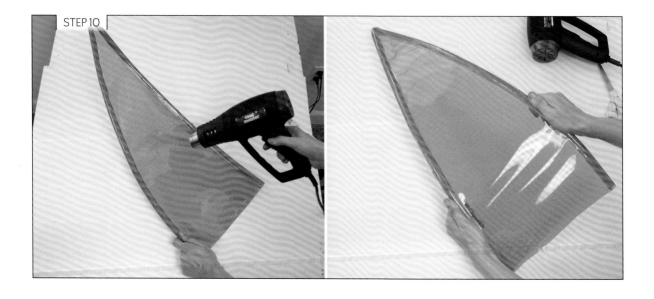

11 | For additional color, PVC Vinyl can be overlaid onto the panel we just created. Carefully lay the vinyl over your panel, and cut the edges as done previously. Cut out any details in this overlay to allow the base color to show through in sections.

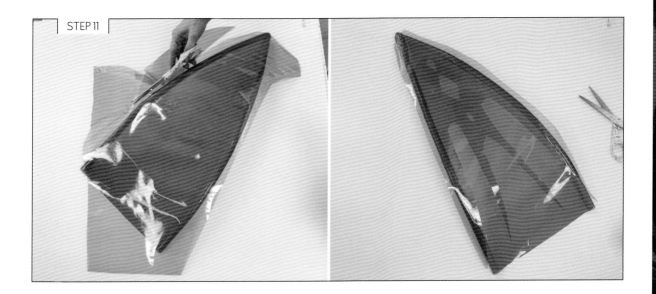

12 | Flip your new overlay piece right side down, and apply a layer of tacky spray glue. Immediately flip this piece over and onto the base panel. Starting from the top, carefully adhere the base and overlay panels together. Pull the edges taut so that both layers of vinyl are flat and smooth.

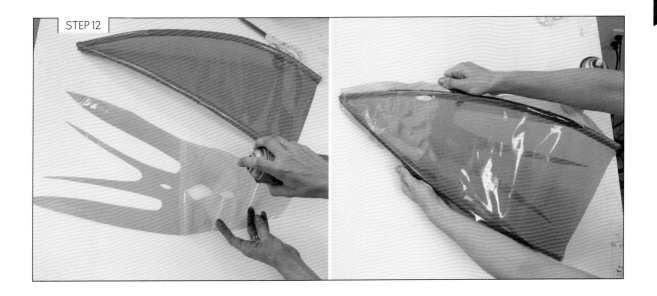

13 | Apply contact cement to the *wrong side* edges of the overlay panel and the framework panel; allow to dry and wrap the overlay edges to adhere to the base panel framework.

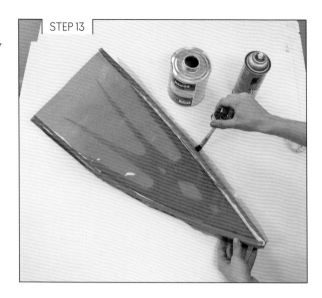

STEP 13

14 | To finish, trim the bottom edge of your panel however you would like the design to look. Apply black acrylic paint on the edges of the framework for neatness.

/ Note / While this example shows the basics for stretching vinyl over a PVC frame, you can use these steps on frames other than plastics, such as aluminum and even wireframing.

STEP 14

Completed wing

Plexi Cosplay
COSPLAYER

Costume Titania (Empress Deluxe skin)
from Digital Extremes' game *Warframe*

Photo by Plexi Cosplay

Plexi Cosplay's Titania (Empress
Deluxe skin) from Digital Extremes'
game *Warframe* utilized an aluminum
framework along with EVA foam and
Plastazote for the top edging.

Plexi Cosplay,
COSPLAYER

**Costume ▸ Astalos Blademaster
from *Monster Hunter Generations***

Photo by Plexi Cosplay

Plexi Cosplay's Astalos armor from
the Capcom® game *Monster Hunter*
utilizes PVC Vinyl for the skirt.

Sintra

What Is Sintra?

Expanded PVC foam, known as Sintra, is a rigid, closed-cell material common in the sign and display industry. Commonly referred to as Sintra (a specific brand name for the material, but there are multiple suppliers), this material is available in a wide array of sizes and thicknesses, making it a great choice for rapid fabrication of rigid components and props.

Uses

Sintra is often used in cosplay to produce armor and props that need to have high rigidity and minimal weight.

Methods of Construction

Expanded PVC is an extremely lightweight and rigid material. Its ability to be shaped with ordinary tools makes it the perfect material for design and display projects. It can be easily sanded, cut, and glued, which is why many use it as a prototyping medium. When heated, it becomes malleable enough to shape into complex, rigid shells for both protection and mounting.

Material Options

Expanded PVC comes in a wide variety of opaque colors and finishes, but is not available in any transparent options. It comes in various thicknesses ranging from ¹⁄₁₆″ to 1″ thick.

Things to Consider

Due to its rigid nature, it has long-lasting durability and is very resistant to higher outdoor temperatures.

⚠️ **SAFETY NOTE:** DO NOT BURN PVC! HEATING AND BURNING PVC CAN RELEASE TOXIC FUMES. YOU SHOULD ALWAYS WEAR A RESPIRATOR AND WORK IN A WELL-VENTILATED AREA.

Frostbite Cosplay

Frostbite Cosplay is a sibling team of artists made up of Aspen, Briston, and Bryce from the Dallas, Texas, area. Frostbite specializes in larger-than-life builds such as Reinhardt, Orisa, and Bastion from Overwatch to a life-sized Toothless from *How To Train Your Dragon*. They do fantastic industry work with many eSports teams, producing mascots, trophies, medals, and other high-quality cosplays and props. Their range of techniques includes 3D modeling/printing, pattern making, sewing, SFX electronics, and hand fabrication of foam and thermoplastics.

Photo by Frostbite Cosplay

FrostBITE

Bryce Eden of Frostbite Cosplay.
COSPLAYER

Costume ▸ Reinhardt (Cobalt skin) from *Overwatch*
Photo by Roxas Studios

Briston Eden of Frostbite Cosplay.
COSPLAYER

Costume ▸ Banbaro Armor Set from *Monster Hunter: World*
Photo by Brett Downen—Downen Photography

MAKING ARMOR TASSETS

by Frostbite Cosplay

This demo is an example of how to create armor tassets using expanded PVC sheets. Sintra and other expanded PVC sheet brands can be used for creating all kinds of rigid armor, props, and other costume pieces!

TOOLS AND MATERIALS

3MM SINTRA OR EXPANDED PVC SHEET

5MM SINTRA OR EXPANDED PVC SHEET

ARMOR PATTERN

SUPER GLUE

UTILITY KNIFE (X-ACTO) OR BOX CUTTER

FINE-TIPPED SHARPIE OR PERMANENT MARKER

HEAT GUN

HEAT-RESISTANT GLOVES

LOW- AND HIGH-GRIT SANDPAPER

AUTOMOTIVE BODY FILLER OR GLAZING AND SPOT PUTTY

PRIMER

PAINT

RIVETS OR CHICAGO SCREWS

RESPIRATOR

/Tip/ Although Sintra can be cut with hand tools, an electric tool such as a band saw will expedite this process.

Instructions

1 | Place your pattern on your Sintra, and with a fine-tipped marker, trace all your armor pieces, where they will be glued, and any overlay details.

| Note | *If your pattern is in halves like in this demo, flip your pattern to mirror the first piece you traced to ensure the symmetry of your armor.*

2 | Cut out your pieces with a utility knife or box cutter. Once the smooth surface plastic is scored, it should cut with minimal force.

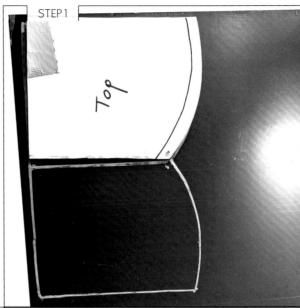

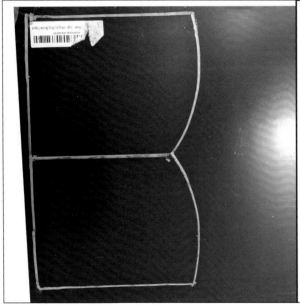

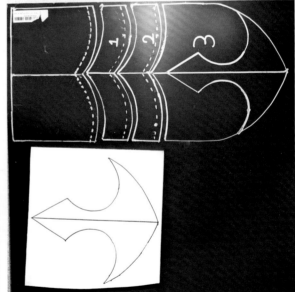

3 | Using your heat gun and heat-resistant gloves, evenly distribute the heat by quickly moving the heat gun over each armor piece until it becomes malleable.

⚠ **SAFETY NOTE:** PVC RELEASES TOXIC FUMES IF OVERHEATED, SO FOR SAFETY, BE SURE YOU'RE WORKING IN A VENTILATED AREA AND YOU WEAR A PROPER RESPIRATOR.

▐Tip▐ You can also heat Sintra by submerging it in boiling water.

4 | With your piece still malleable, crease it using an edged surface like a table to ensure straight and consistent shaping.

▐Tip▐ If you're trying to create curved shapes, you can use metal mixing bowls or cylinders for this step.

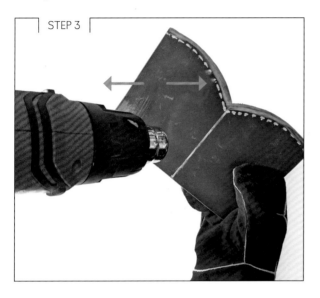

STEP 3

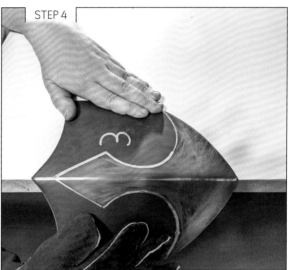

STEP 4

5 | Once all your armor elements have been shaped and are cool to the touch, glue all the pieces together with Super Glue. If you're using a two-part epoxy, you will need to let it cure for the time recommended on the packaging.

6 | After your glue has set, fill any gaps between your connecting pieces with automotive body filler, glazing and spot putty, or both if necessary.

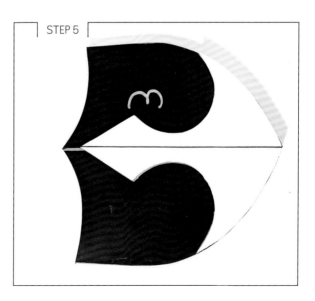

STEP 5

7 | Once the fillers are dry, start sanding down these areas. Begin with lower-grit sandpaper (around 120 grit is recommended) and work your way up to a higher grit (400 or higher) until your desired smoothness is achieved.

8 | Use a marker to indicate where you want your rivets to be placed on your armor piece. Drill each mark with a bit that matches the diameter of your rivet.

9 | Coat all assembled pieces with a urethane filler primer. You may have to apply multiple coats if you still notice sanding scratches. Once dry, sand until smooth with a higher-grit sandpaper (800 or higher).

STEP 7

Armor after being filled and sanded

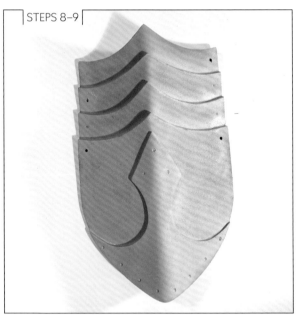

STEPS 8–9

10 | Complete your armor by painting it with the paint of your choosing. For this demo, airbrush paints were used.

11 | Install the rivets into the armor to finish your piece. For this demo, the top two holes in the armor were utilized to attach the piece to a belt.

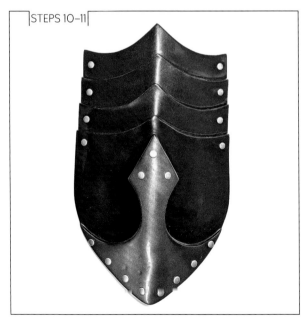

STEPS 10–11

Finished armor
tasset

Polygon Forge

Polygon Forge is an award-winning cosplayer from Switzerland. She is known for her unique low-polygon creations, making cosplays that look like digital computer art. She loves developing new fabrication techniques and uses a variety of materials such as Sintra, polystyrene, and vinyl wraps. Polygon Forge was the 2021 Ultimate Online Cosplay Championship Best in Show Winner, and we are proud to showcase her demonstrations.

Costume ▸ **Master Chief from** *Halo*

Photo by Seelenfang

Costume ▸ **Tyto the Swift from** *Gigantic*

Photos by Céline Stucki

BUILDING A LOW-POLY MASK

by Polygon Forge

Sintra is also known as expanded PVC foam. It is solid and lightweight, has a smooth surface, and comes in various colors and thicknesses. Sintra, compared to other thermoplastics, is on the more brittle side, so keep this in mind when planning what you will make. This tutorial will show you how to use car vinyl wraps to cover and protect the material.

TOOLS AND MATERIALS

SINTRA (AROUND ⅒″ THICK, USE A MATCHING COLOR IF AVAILABLE)

CAR VINYL WRAPS (IN 2 COLORS)

SUPER GLUE

PAPER OR FINISHED PATTERNS

TRANSPARENT REMOVABLE TAPE

METAL RULER

SCISSORS

BOX CUTTER

CUTTING MAT

HEAT GUN

DUAL-FILTER RESPIRATOR

EYE PROTECTION

DISPOSABLE GLOVES

SANDPAPER (60 AND 180 GRIT)

SANDING BLOCK (OPTIONAL)

PAPER TOWELS

PEN OR PENCIL

Instructions

1 | Using your ruler and pencil, draw a simple mask pattern using geometric shapes. Label each piece of your pattern systematically. If two neighboring pieces meet at an angle pointing outward, indicate that the cut needs to be beveled. Take a photo or photocopy to refer back to for later reassembly.

2 | Cut out your pattern pieces with scissors before using them with your car vinyl. Leaving roughly 1˝ around your pattern, cut out the vinyl.

3 | Tape the pattern to a Sintra sheet with transparent tape.

STEP 1

STEP 2

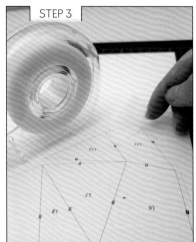

STEP 3

4 | Use the box cutter and ruler to cut out each pattern piece over your cutting mat. For bevel cuts, hold the box cutter at an angle, but otherwise, maintain a straight edge. It takes a few cuts to get all the way through the material. Make sure you label the back of each piece as you cut, or keep the cut-out patterns on top of the pieces for reference. Otherwise, reassembly can get tricky!

STEP 4

5 | Assemble all pieces of the mask by sticking transparent tape to the outside. Use the photo of the pattern as a reference if necessary. Some pieces may not fit if there is too much material on the inside of a bevel. Remove the excess material by carving it off with a box cutter or using low-grit sandpaper (recommended 60 grit).

⚠ **SAFETY NOTE:** ALWAYS WEAR A DUST MASK OR RESPIRATOR WITH COMBINATION FILTERS AND EYE PROTECTION WHEN SANDING.

STEP 5

6 | Carefully apply an adequate amount of glue into all seams on the inside of the mask. If some glue spills to the out-facing side, immediately wipe it off with a paper towel.

⚠ **SAFETY NOTE:** WEAR DISPOSABLE GLOVES, A RESPIRATOR, AND EYE PROTECTION WHEN WORKING WITH THIS KIND OF GLUE.

7 | After the glue sets, remove the transparent tape.

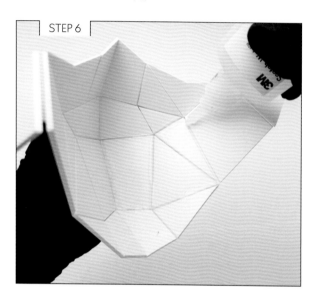

STEP 6

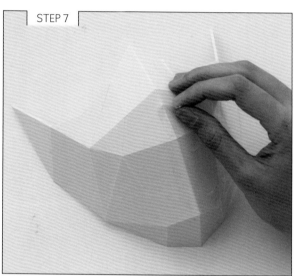

STEP 7

8 | If any glue is set on the out-facing side of your mask, carefully sand it away with sandpaper (recommended 180 grit or higher).

/Tip/ You can use a sanding block to ensure your geometric edges stay sharp.

Once your mask's surface is perfectly smooth, clean your work area, mask, and hands of any dust particles.

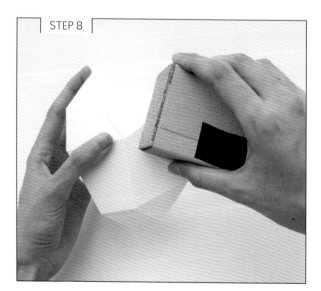

STEP 8

9 | Starting from one end of your mask, peel off the corresponding end of your vinyl, and apply it to this first section. Gently rub this section down with your fingers, and continue to peel the vinyl backing away as you slowly move along the mask, rubbing back and forth until it is fully covered.

/ Tip / *You can use a dull object to get the vinyl into harder-to-reach areas.*

/ Note / *If bubbles form under the vinyl as you're applying, carefully peel it back and reapply it. If the vinyl won't bend to your will, you may have to cut and apply it in smaller pieces.*

STEP 9

10 | Use your scissors to cut the remaining vinyl at 90° angles toward each edge. Flip them down to the back side of the mask to secure the vinyl.

11 | Tape the detail pattern pieces onto your second color choice of vinyl, and with a ruler and box cutter, cut them out. Apply the vinyl by repeating the techniques from Step 9.

STEP 10

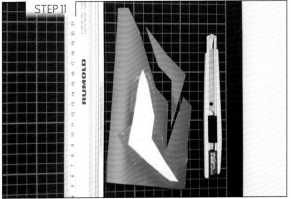

STEP 11

12 | To set the vinyl, treat the finished mask with a heat gun. Too much heat can warp Sintra, so make sure to first test the proper heat setting on a scrap piece of Sintra wrapped in vinyl. Gently rub over the warmed-up mask. Use a bit of extra pressure at sharp angles so they stay applied even when the material has cooled down. You can reheat the mask or parts of it multiple times.

⚠ SAFETY NOTE: WEAR A RESPIRATOR AND WORK IN A WELL-VENTILATED AREA WHEN HEATING THE MATERIALS, AS THE VAPORS ARE TOXIC. BE CAUTIOUS; THE PIECES GET HOT TO THE TOUCH IF TOO MUCH HEAT IS USED.

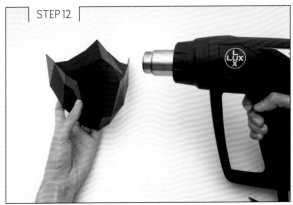

STEP 12

13 | Now it's time to glue on some elastic straps, and from there you're done! Allow your Super Glue to cure for a full 24 hours before you wear your mask.

/Note/ With this method, not only can you build geometric shapes with Sintra; you also can bend it into angles or curves. The surface can be carved or painted.

STEP 13

Completed mask

Polygon Forge,
COSPLAYER

**Costume ▶ Gods within Steel
Undead Trial Anubis Statue**

Photo by Seelenfang

Polygon Forge's Anubis costume
is made almost entirely out of
car vinyl–wrapped Sintra.

◎ Styrene

What Is Styrene?

Also known as HIPS (High Impact Polystyrene), Styrene is a thermoforming plastic. It is one of the most popular thermoplastics available for industrial use. It is extremely easy to vacuum form and shape when heated. Styrene is nontoxic and odorless.

Uses

Styrene is commonly used for models, prototypes, displays, enclosures, costumes, and prop making.

Methods of Construction

Styrene can be shaped, drilled, sawed, sheared, punched, vacuum formed, laser cut, machined, and painted. It can be scored and snapped to create straight lines, but this often leaves extremely sharp corners.

Styrene Options

It is naturally opaque and comes in both black and white colors.

⚠ **SAFETY NOTE:** THERMOPLASTICS MAY BE VERY HOT TO THE TOUCH WHEN HEATED. USE PROTECTIVE GLOVES OR WAIT FOR THE MATERIAL TO COOL DOWN BEFORE HANDLING. USE A SMALL BOWL OF COOL WATER TO DIP YOUR FINGERS IN BEFORE HANDLING THE PRODUCT.

SEE MORE
INFORMATION
*about Polygon
Forge on
page 122.*

STYRENE DEMO 1

CREATING POLYGONAL FABRIC

by Polygon Forge

This demo shows how to make a phone pouch using polystyrene as a base material. The same technique can be used to create more complex pieces like clothing.

TOOLS AND MATERIALS

STYRENE SHEET (⁴⁄₁₀₀″ THICK)

CAR VINYL WRAP

COTTON JERSEY FABRIC (IN THE SAME COLOR AS THE VINYL)

NEEDLE AND THREAD (IN MATCHING COLOR)

SUPER GLUE

2 SMALL NEODYMIUM MAGNETS

PAPER

TRANSPARENT TAPE

METAL RULER

SCISSORS

BOX CUTTER

CUTTING MAT

HEAT GUN

DUAL–FILTER RESPIRATOR

SAFETY GLASSES

DISPOSABLE GLOVES

SANDPAPER (60 AND 180 GRIT)

DUCT TAPE

MASKING TAPE

WATERPROOF PEN

Instructions

1 | Make a pattern for the pouch by tracing the outline of your phone onto a sheet of paper, then draw a polygonal pattern inside. Add a triangle on top to close the pouch. Draw a second pattern for the front side, then label each piece of the pattern systematically. Take a photo or photocopy for easier reassembling later.

2 | Roughly cut around the pattern with scissors, then tape the pattern to a styrene sheet with transparent tape.

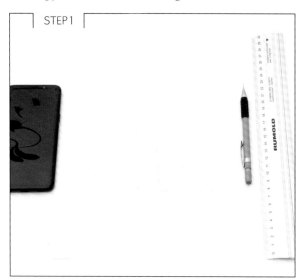

STEP 1

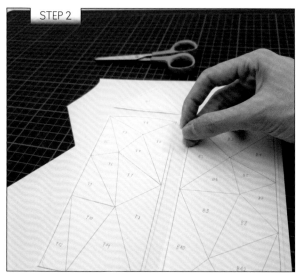

STEP 2

3 | Use the box cutter and ruler to cut out each individual piece. It takes multiple cuts to get through the material. Keep your blade tip sharp by occasionally snapping off a piece. Label the backs of the pieces with a pen while working; it's easiest if you flip them over as if in a mirror and label them at that exact angle so all labels face up when reassembling later.

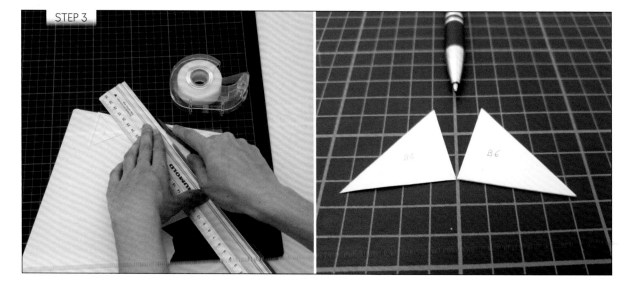

STEP 3

4 | Tape down pieces of 60- and 180-grit sandpaper with duct tape. Slightly sand the front-side edges of each piece until they don't stick out anymore, using the rough sandpaper first and finishing with the smoother grit.

⚠ **SAFETY NOTE:** ALWAYS WEAR A DUST MASK OR RESPIRATOR WITH COMBINATION FILTERS AND EYE PROTECTION WHEN SANDING.

STEP 4

5 | Clean the sanded pieces with water, and let them dry.

6 | Put the pieces onto the vinyl, and cut around them with scissors, leaving a bit of margin around every piece.

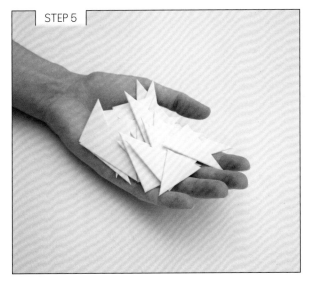
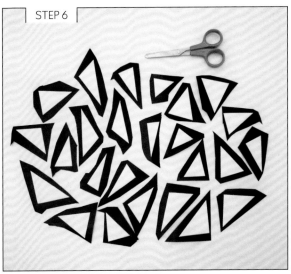

STEP 5

STEP 6

7 | One piece at a time, peel off the vinyl's protective cover, and stick it to one edge of your styrene piece. Rub back and forth from that starting point until it's fully adhered.

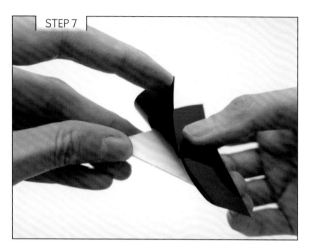

STEP 7

8 | Cut at 90° angles toward each edge with scissors. Fold and stick the resulting flaps to the back of each piece. Cut off excess vinyl, and make sure the label on the back side remains visible.

STEP 8

9 | Heat seal all pieces with a heat gun so the vinyl sets. Make sure to first test the proper heat setting on a scrap styrene piece wrapped in vinyl.

⚠ **SAFETY NOTE:** WEAR A RESPIRATOR AND WORK IN A WELL-VENTILATED AREA WHEN HEATING THE MATERIALS, AS THE VAPORS ARE TOXIC. BE CAUTIOUS; THE PIECES GET HOT TO THE TOUCH IF TOO MUCH HEAT IS USED.

STEP 9

10 | Turn all pieces so their backs are facing up, and arrange them according to their labels. Use the photo of the pattern as a reference if necessary. Note the pattern looks flipped while the back sides are up. Then tape the pieces together with transparent tape, and flip it all over to right side up.

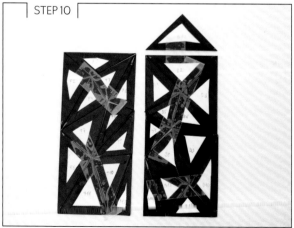

STEP 10

11 | Cut a strip of cotton jersey large enough for all the pieces. Peel the pieces off the tape, and lay them on the fabric.

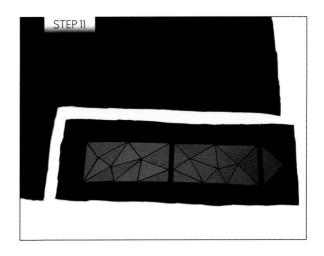

STEP 11

12 | Add glue to a piece's borders, press the piece onto the fabric for a few seconds, then continue with the neighboring piece. Leave a gap as thick as your phone between the front and back sides of the pouch and a slightly larger gap before the triangular flap.

⚠ **SAFETY NOTE:** WEAR DISPOSABLE GLOVES, A RESPIRATOR, AND EYE PROTECTION WHEN WORKING WITH THIS KIND OF GLUE.

STEP 12

13 | Cut away most excess fabric with scissors, but leave enough to hand sew the sides together. Fold the extra fabric to the inside of the pouch, then use small hand stitches in matching thread to close both sides.

STEP 13

14 | Cover the surface in masking tape. Fold and glue in the overhanging fabric where the pouch opens, using as little glue as possible.

STEP 14

15 Glue on the magnets. Leave the pouch alone for a few days so the Super Glue can fully cure, then remove the masking tape.

STEP 15

You are finished! The same method can be used to create gauntlets, trousers, and other pieces of clothing. For complex pieces, making the patterns using 3D software is advised.

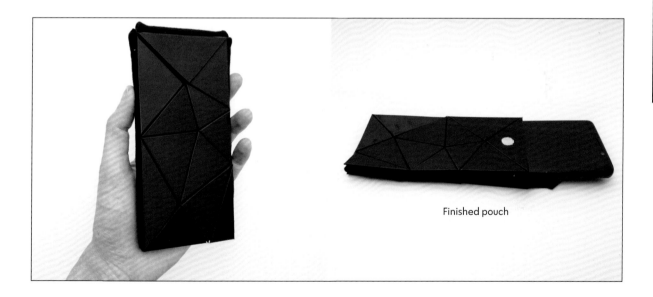

Finished pouch

Polygon Forge,
COSPLAYER

Costume   Tyto the Swift from
Gigantic

Photo by Céline Stucki Photography

Polygon Forge's Tyto the Swift cos‐
tume from the game *Gigantic* uses
polygonal fabric for almost every
piece. Notably, the trousers, shirt,
boots, and gauntlet are all made
with polygonal fabric.

Acrylic Solids

What Is Acrylic?

Acrylic is a thermoforming plastic that is naturally transparent, offering glass-like clarity and luster while being substantially stronger at a fraction of the cost and weight of glass.

Uses

This material is commonly used to make lenses, security barriers, paint, furniture, medical devices, and LCD screens.

Methods of Construction

Acrylic is great for cosplay and can be used to make visors, props, and even wings. Cast acrylic sheets can be cut and engraved safely with CO_2 lasers and desktop CNC routers to create precise rigid parts as well as transparent components and effects.

Acrylic Options

Acrylic is sold in a variety of colors, including fluorescent colors. Acrylic (or poly[methyl methacrylate]) is available in a wide variety of colors, thicknesses, and sizes, making it an extremely versatile material for costume and prop fabrication. Some manufacturers even produce special surface texture finishes.

Things to Consider

Acrylic can shatter when enough force is applied; compared to alternatives such as PETG.

⚠ **SAFETY NOTE:** THERMOPLASTICS MAY BE VERY HOT TO THE TOUCH WHEN HEATED. USE PROTECTIVE GLOVES OR WAIT FOR THE MATERIAL TO COOL DOWN BEFORE HANDLING. ACRYLIC SPECIFICALLY RETAINS HEAT FOR SUBSTANTIALLY LONGER AMOUNTS OF TIME COMPARED TO OTHER THERMOPLASTICS.

ACRYLIC SOLIDS DEMO 1
DAGGER PROP
● by Frostbite Cosplay ●

SEE MORE INFORMATION *about Frostbite Cosplay on page 116.*

MATERIAL LIST

12MM CAST ACRYLIC SHEET

2MM CAST ACRYLIC SHEET

ACRYLIC CEMENT OR CYANOACRYLATE GLUE

ROTARY TOOL

SANDPAPER

PAINT

LEATHER WRAP

Instructions

1 | Design the desired shapes using computer illustration and tool control programs.

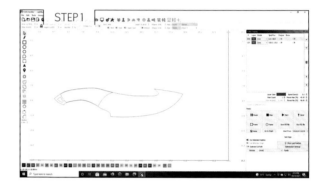

2 | Cut the acrylic material using a laser or CNC router. Cutting time and settings will vary depending on the equipment used.

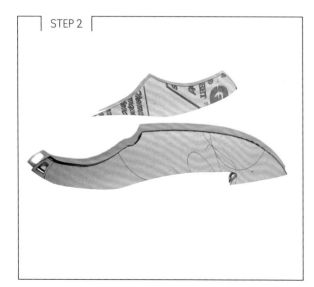

3 | If cyanoacrylate glue is being used, sand the parts to allow for a better bond. If using acrylic cement, skip this step.

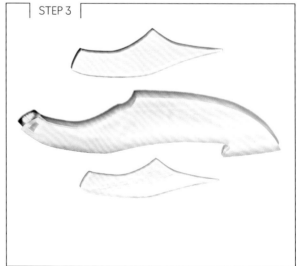

4 | Glue the parts into place, and give the glue time to cure.

5 | Use a rotary tool to shape and smooth the edges. Round the bottom as well as the tip of the blade, instead of sharpening, for safety. Sand it completely with high-grit sandpaper to improve paint bonding.

⚠ **SAFETY NOTE:** ALWAYS WEAR A DUST MASK OR RESPIRATOR AND EYE PROTECTION WHEN SANDING OR USING AN ELECTRIC ROTARY TOOL.

STEP 4

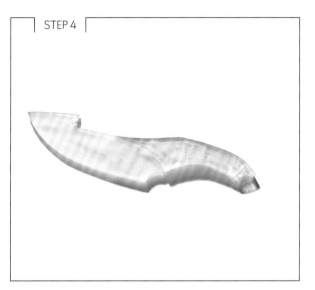

STEP 5

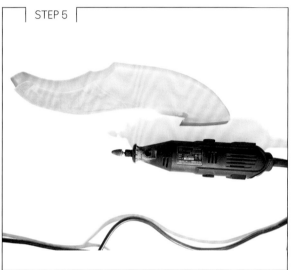

6 | Prime and paint the prop.

7 | Finish the handle of this knife with a leather wrap. Make it as simple or complex as desired.

/ Note / *This tutorial shows steps for a simple painted rigid prop, but the knife could easily be left transparent or fitted with LEDs for special effects.*

STEP 7

Hoku Props

Hoku Props is led by propmaker Chad Hoku and seamstress Sammy Hoku. Chad's background in 3D has him designing cosplays digitally before utilizing different fabrication techniques to make armor, props, and all kinds of costume components. Sammy's love for cosplay at a young age led her to study fashion/costume design as an adult, and she uses this knowledge to cover all sewn elements for Hoku Props's cosplay projects. Hoku Props is best known for its Lionhardt cosplay, which won Grand Prize at TwitchCon's first Cosplay Contest in 2016 and for cofounding the Ultimate Online Cosplay Championship in 2020 with Tock Custom.

Sammy of Hoku Props,
COSPLAYER

B

A

Chad of Hoku Props,
COSPLAYER

A | Costume   Reinhardt (Lionhardt
skin) from *Overwatch*; wig/beard
by Malinda "Malinda Chan" Mathis

Photo by Alexandra Lee Studios

B | Costume ▶ Tohsaka Rin from *Fate/
stay night*

Photo by Hoku Props

C | Costume ▶ Trevor Belmont and
Sypha Belnades from *Castlevania*
(Animated Series)

Photo by Alexandra Lee Studios

ACRYLIC SOLIDS DEMO 2

LASER CUTTING ACRYLIC

by Hoku Props

Automated machining is something that can really elevate your hobby or help your small business grow, and with laser cutters becoming more affordable in recent years, any maker should consider adding one to their arsenal. This demo will give you an inside peek into the basics of laser cutting with various materials.

What Is CO2 Laser Cutting?

Laser cutting is the process of energizing CO_2 gas trapped inside a glass tube. When electrical energy is introduced, it causes the CO_2 molecules to energize and, as they collide, produce a significant amount of infrared light. As this light bounces inside the tube and continues to collide with the CO_2, it creates a chain reaction that results in a concentrated beam. This laser tube is designed to allow the concentrated beam to escape through a small porthole where mirrors are used to direct the light toward a focusing lens. The focusing lens is like a precision magnifying glass and collects all the rays of light into a small point called a beam spot. The beam spot in focus is typically .004″ in width. Because of how focused this beam is, it carries a tremendous amount of energy, which allows it to burn/melt through any burnable material. When this laser is combined with motors and computer-controlled programs, we can achieve very accurate and repeatable cutting and etching results in minimal time.

Uses

• Easily replicating foam/fabric patterns

• Repeatable test cutting on various materials

• Creating flexible properties in rigid materials

• Etching and engraving

• Cutting materials with minimal cleanup

• So much more

Adobe Illustrator is industry-level software that is used to create vector designs and graphics. We use it to design vectors that will be used to generate cutting paths for the laser cutter called a tool path.

Most laser cutting issues start and end with software, which often lacks support for the essential quality-of-life features present in more suitable software. LightBurn is an aftermarket laser-cutting suite that solves this problem by supporting many machines on the market with pre-made profiles, so it's essentially plug and play. Best of all, LightBurn supports most premier features found in very

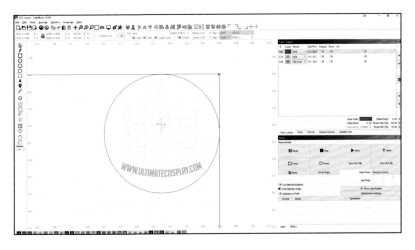

expensive competitors. These improvements include camera-guided systems, vector layers where you can set cutting order, custom power and speed settings, rastering, global home, and relative home.

The settings that are highlighted correspond with the cutting action that you intend. This is where you can select the type of cut by choosing fill or line. The next variable is speed, which represents the rate at which the laser head travels. The last variable is power, which represents the amount of energy that is being sent to the laser tube. There are several points to consider. A very slow-moving

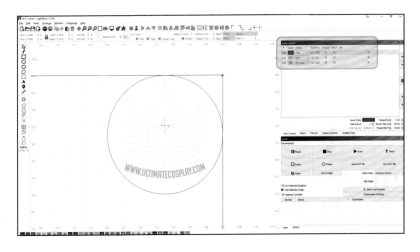

tool path with a very low power setting can cut through an object. A quick-moving laser cutter with very high power can also cut through an object. Our goal is to find the balance between these two standards. The speed and power settings often depend on the precision and delicacy of the cut as well as the overall power capacity of your laser tube. A final consideration is that each laser cutter has a sweet spot. Higher-powered laser tubes often struggle to output low ranges of power, resulting in excessive cutting action and poor detail cuts and engravings. Again, balance is key and should be considered before deciding on how powerful your laser needs to be. If you are interested in a good balance, look for a model that has a 70-watt to 90-watt laser tube.

Laser cutters typically come with two types of beds: honeycomb and blades. Honeycomb is what we have on our laser cutter in this demo. The major benefit of honeycomb is that even relatively small pieces won't fall through and potentially be damaged or lost. Blades are often found on large-sized industrial machines.

A laser cutter's working environment is controlled as an X and Y grid with coordinates. When you first boot up your device, it will travel (jog) to the origin (0,0) of X and Y so it can establish a home location. This is referred to as the global home.

In this photo, the laser cutter is performing a low-powered border cut of the blue vector shown in LightBurn. You always want to save the full border cut for the very end. This test is to ensure the material is big enough for the entire cut.

/ Pro Tip! / *This is where having a camera system in Light-Burn can be of great benefit since it shows you a mock up of the cut on your material before you start cutting.*

One type of cut is called a raster engrave. This type of cut occurs along the interior of a vector and is what you would use to perform a clearance or sweeping-style cutting action.

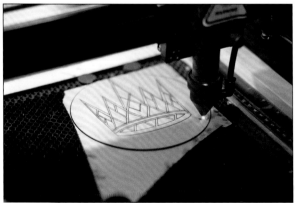

See in the picture how the interior of each letter has been etched away. This is a raster engraving.

The other type of cut is called a vector cut/engrave. This type of cut occurs along the profile of a vector and is what you would use to create hairline engraving and cutting actions.

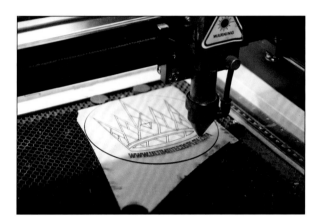

This is our final piece with the protective film still on. The film is there to prevent the plastic surrounding the cut from being damaged by stray laser light and super-heated plastic.

Various finished pieces of differing materials

DYEING PLASTICS

SEE MORE
INFORMATION
*about Hoku Props
on page 143.*

● by Hoku Props ●

In this tutorial, we'll show you how to color clear acrylic plastic with synthetic dyes. Acrylic has many common uses today because of its natural transparency and impact-resistant qualities. Although we show the dyeing process only using acrylic in our examples, this process can be used to color other plastics, such as PETG.

TOOLS AND MATERIALS

ACRYLIC OR PETG

RIT DYEMORE SYNTHETIC DYE

WATER

LARGE MIXING BOWL

METAL TONGS OR METAL COAT HANGER

LARGE POT

STOVE TOP OR HOT PLATE

LATEX OR VINYL GLOVES

TRASH BAG OR PLASTIC SHEET

1 | Set up your dyeing station. Depending on your workspace, protect the surface with either a plastic sheet or a trash bag. Next, fill your mixing bowl with room-temperature water. This mainly will be used to cool down your plastics; however, you'll also be using it to add more water to the pot as your dye mixture evaporates. Be sure to use a bowl that can be ruined, as you should not use it for food after it is in contact with the dye.

2 | Since this process involves boiling water, you'll need to use either metal tongs or create a rack by deforming a wire coat hanger to suspend the plastic pieces. You don't want any burned fingers! We created our rack by bending an aluminum welding rod, but a metal coat hanger can be used just the same. You can use either; the primary aim for this is safety.

3 | Add your water to the pot. We are using 8 cups for our red dye here, but depending on the color and shade you're trying to achieve, the amount of water and bottles of dye you need may vary. We recommend 8 cups of water per bottle of dye for strong and vibrant color saturation. It's important to record the volumes and ratios of both water and dye so you have a reference point for repeatability in the future.

4 | Now thoroughly shake your bottle of dye, and pour the entire contents into the pot as it is coming to temperature. Stir your mixture to ensure the dye completely incorporates with the water.

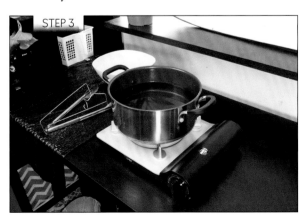

5 | Before you start dyeing any major costume pieces, you're going to need to run some tests to determine the number of dyeing intervals you need to perform to achieve your desired color. For our tests, we used both squares and mini–Ultimate Cosplay crowns, but any scrap pieces of the same thickness as your final costume piece will do.

6 | Put on your latex or vinyl gloves to protect your hands from the dye. Turn your heating element up until the dye mixture begins to boil. Once it's boiling, turn the heat down until the mixture maintains a low simmer (when the liquid has slight movement on the surface and bubbles rarely). Now it's time to start submerging our test pieces into our dye mixture at timed intervals.

7 | Take one of your test pieces, and submerge it into your dye for 30 seconds.

STEP 5

STEP 7

8 | Transfer this piece to your room-temperature water for 3 to 5 seconds; it's important that you only reduce the temperature as letting the piece cool completely will fully set the dye. After the quick dip in the room-temperature water, inspect your test piece to ensure that the material isn't warping from the heat.

If your test piece has maintained its shape, repeat this process until you reach the shade you're aiming for.

However, if your piece has warped like in this picture, start with a new test piece, and reduce your submerge time until you no longer experience warping. This may take a few tries and possibly different times. Patience is going to be key during these tests!

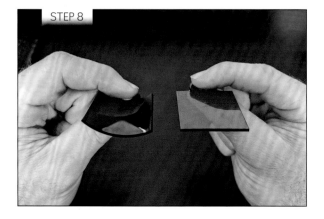

STEP 8

9 | Once you have reached the shade you're going for, let your test piece cool completely in your bowl of room-temperature water.

Repeat this test every time you use a new material and every time you use a different thickness. Test this process with 3 to 5 pieces so you will have color and shade references to use for future dyeing projects.

Finished dyed pieces

10 | Now that you have determined the number of intervals it will take to dye your plastic, you can move on to your main costume piece while following these same steps. Depending on the size of your piece, you may have to use a larger pot/heat-safe container to hold your dye mixture, and you'll have to incorporate more water/dye.

/Tip/ These dyes can be mixed to create custom colors. For example, if you wanted to dye your plastic a specific shade of purple, you could use a combination of blue and red dye to attain this. You will need to experiment if you're looking for a very specific shade. However, you can find an extensive mixing chart on Rit's website.

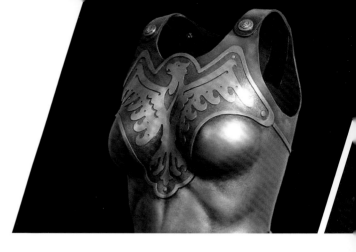

Vacu-Forming

What Is Vacuum Forming/Vacu-Forming?

Vacuum forming is a method used to shape plastic materials. For this process, a sheet of thermoplastic or EVA foam is heated and then pulled around a positive form using suction.

Uses

Vacuum forming is great when you need to make identical copies of the same object. You can use a wide variety of materials, and it is especially useful when you need to keep things lightweight.

Vacu-Forming Material Options

- EVA foam
- PETG
- Styrene
- Acrylic
- ABS

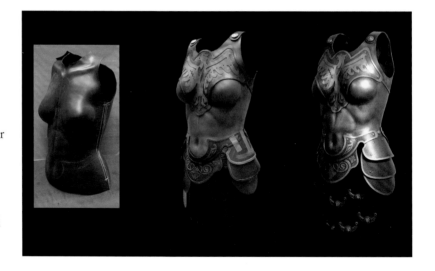

Things to Consider

- Never leave your vacuum former unattended. The timing of the steps is very important.

- Vacuum forming is moderately difficult. Don't get discouraged if it doesn't go well the first time.

⚠ **SAFETY NOTES**

- VACUUM FORMING USES VERY HIGH HEAT. MAKE SURE YOU WEAR HEAT-RESISTANT GLOVES.

- ALWAYS VACUUM FORM IN A WELL-VENTILATED AREA, AND WEAR A RESPIRATOR.

Prop Monkey Studio

Dave Kramer of Prop Monkey Studio is a traditional fine art painter, cosplayer, and specialty product manufacturer from Dallas, Texas. As a freelance artist of 30 years, Dave has found success working on illustrations, book covers, oil painting, sculpting, photography, lifecasting, prop making, costume design, and so much more. He and his son founded Prop Monkey Studio in 2019 to produce products that help artists create more refined costumes.

AMAZON WARRIOR ARMOR

Even though vacuum forming is meant for mass production, I always thought it could be used for individual cosplay to increase quality and speed up production. Several years ago I set out to show the costume and prop-building community that this is a viable solution to many issues when working with foam and plastics.

Make a Vacuum Former

I've built seven or eight vacuum-forming setups, from 10″ × 12″ to 24″ × 36″ (25cm × 30cm to 61cm × 92cm). This 18″ × 24″ (46cm × 61cm) is my favorite. I like it because it does a lot of what I need it to do but doesn't take up much space. Here are the plans for it.

18″ × 24″ Vacuum Former Table

TOOLS AND MATERIALS

WOOD STRIP (1″ × 2″ × 8′)

SHEET OF ½″-THICK MDF BOARD (24″ × 24″)

SHEET OF ¼″-THICK MDF BOARD (24″ × 24″)

RUBBER PIMPLE MAT (12″ × 18″)

SHEET OF 4MM HIGH-DENSITY EVA FOAM (24″ × 18″)

WOOD GLUE

HOLE CUTTING BIT

CAN OF PERMANENT ADHESIVE SPRAY

Instructions

1 | Cut one ½″-thick MDF board 18″ × 24″ and cut one ¼″-thick MDF board 18″ × 24″.

2 | Cut the long 1″ × 2″ × 8′ foot board into two 24″ sections, and two 16½″ sections.

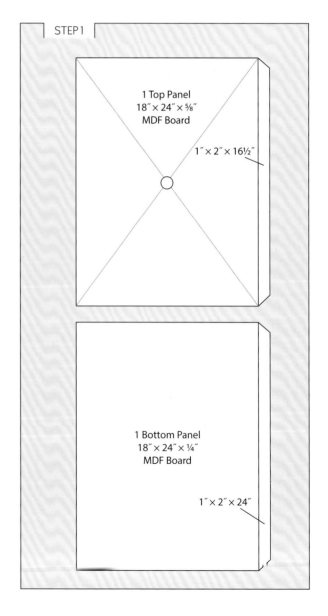

STEP 1

1 Top Panel
18″ × 24″ × ⅝″
MDF Board

1″ × 2″ × 16½″

1 Bottom Panel
18″ × 24″ × ¼″
MDF Board

1″ × 2″ × 24″

3 | Glue and clamp one 1″ × 2″ × 24″ section to the top (½″ thick) panel. Then, glue and clamp the two 16½″ sections to either side of the same top panel.

4 | Before attaching the last 24″ section, use your hole cutting bit to drill a hole in the center of this section.

/ Cutting Holes / *Use your vacuum cleaner hose to see what size hole you need to drill. I used a 1¼″ hole bit for my vacuum hose.*

5 | Glue and clamp the final drilled section to the top board.

6 | Drill a hole in the center of the top panel and then glue and clamp the bottom (¼″ thick) panel to the opposite side.

7 | Once the MDF panels are assembled and drilled, prepare your sheet of EVA foam by cutting it into a 1½″ thick frame. Use your adhesive spray to adhere your EVA foam frame to the top panel of the forming table.

8 | Cut a hole in the center of your pimple mat with a utility knife. You do not need to permanently attach this to the MDF.

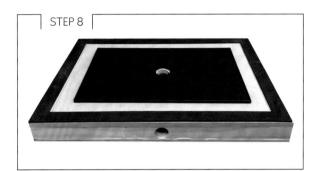

STEP 8

18″ × 24″ Vacuum Former Frame Guide

TOOLS AND MATERIALS

LEFT OVER SCRAPS

Instructions

Using left over scraps, I was able to make this frame guide. This comes in handy when trying to find the correct position during vacuum forming.

Made with 2½″ wide strips of ¼″-thick MDF board. It does not attach to the forming table, but just slide it under and it will be held in place by the weight of the table.

18" × 24" Vacuum Former Frame

TOOLS AND MATERIALS

SHEET OF ¼"-THICK MDF BOARD (24" × 48")

1¼" × 72" × ⅛"-THICK ALUMINUM ANGLE

WOOD GLUE

WOOD SCREWS

CONTACT CEMENT

BOX OF BINDER CLIPS

SANDING BELTS (PACK OF 5), 3" × 21", 30–40 GRIT (FOR WORKING WITH EVA FOAM)

HEAT-SAFE RUBBER (FOR WORKING WITH ABS, PETG, OR HIPS)

3 | Attach the aluminum angles to the long sides of each frame. Use your binder clips to hold the 2 frames together; 5 clips on either side should hold material in place nicely.

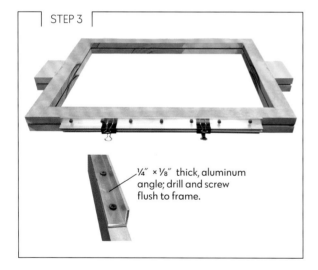

STEP 3

¼" × ⅛" thick, aluminum angle; drill and screw flush to frame.

Instructions

1 | Cut two 24" × 18" × ¾" MDF boards. Then, plunge cut with a table saw or use a circular saw to create a 1½"-thick frame. Then, attach some hand grips on either side using scrap materials and wood glue/screws)

2 | Cut the ¾"-thick aluminum angle into four 18" sections. Drill 7 holes evenly spaced out into the aluminum angle sections.

/ Very Important / *Pre-drill holes into the wood panels and make sure the aluminum angles are perfectly flush to the side of the frame.*

4 | Cut the sanding belts or heat safe rubber into 1½" strips. Trim and glue down with contact cement to the inside of each frame, as shown below. This will grip the material tightly in the frame when vacuum forming.

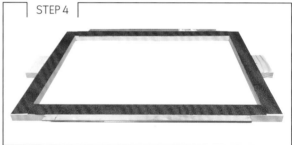

STEP 4

5 | You may need to add screws near each frame handle and hand clamps for extra grip for working with EVA foam. This will help get a more balanced result.

Optional: If you plan to vacuum form both EVA foam and other plastic materials, you may want to make 2 sets of frames; one lined with sanding belts, and one with heat safe rubber.

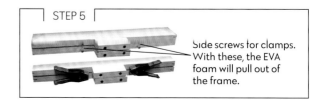

STEP 5

Side screws for clamps. With these, the EVA foam will pull out of the frame.

18″ × 24″ Vacuum Former Heater Trough

TOOLS AND MATERIALS

WOOD STRIP (1″ × 2″ × 4′)

SHEET OF ¼″-THICK MDF BOARD (24″ × 48″)

HEAVY DUTY ALUMINUM FOIL

CAN OF PERMANENT ADHESIVE SPRAY

WOOD GLUE

WOOD SCREWS

COMFORT ZONE CZQTV5M CEILING MOUNT QUARTZ HEATER, BLACK, 1500 WATTS (OR SIMILAR HEATING UNIT)

Instructions

1 | Cut all panels of MDF:

- 2 MDF side panels (11″ × 24″)

- 2 MDF end panels (12″ × 17″ with a 12″ × 3½″ slot cut in the bottoms)

- 4 wood support strips (12″ × 17″)

2 | Assemble the heater trough completely before adding the foil. Mark lines on the MDF where the foil should be applied.

3 | Disassemble the panels and adhere the heavy duty foil inside the marked areas of the MDF. Spray adhesive spray to the dull side of the foil when attaching. The foil can overlap as needed. Using a rubber roller can be helpful.

4 | Reassemble the panels, using wood glue and screws as needed to complete the unit.

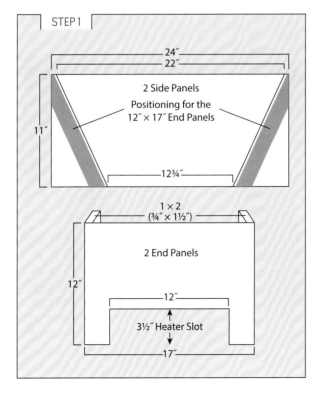

STEP 1

24″
22″

2 Side Panels
Positioning for the
12″ × 17″ End Panels

11″

12¾″

1 × 2
(¾″ × 1½″)

2 End Panels

12″

12″

3½″ Heater Slot

17″

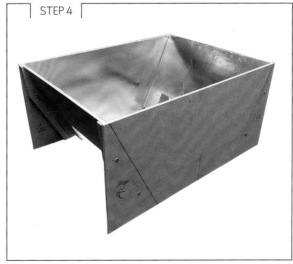

STEP 4

Vacuum Forming

The Buck

The pattern (or buck) is the hardest thing to make for this process, but once you have that, you can use it over and over again to quickly knock out seamless, accurate, foundational shapes for all sorts of builds. You can even modify the pattern by adding temporary shapes to your buck. Think of it this way: In minutes, you can form a foundational shape that would have taken you one to three days to build, and on top of that you'll have little to no need for seam filling.

The buck needs to be strong enough to withstand the pressure of the vacuum forming. I have had some patterns get crushed. I usually use Hydrocal plaster, wood, or reinforced plastic for my bucks.

I have used plasticine sculpting clay for a one-time buck. It must spend a few hours in the freezer to help it hold up to the high temperatures of the vacuum-forming process. It gets a bit messy when you pull the clay out.

A temperature-measuring device is not essential. I vacuum formed for years before getting one, but it is nice to know how hot your unit can get. I've reached temperatures of 400°F (200°C) on this 18″ × 24″ unit.

Here is how I have my 18″ × 24″ unit set up. It's on a low table with enough room between the heating unit and vacuum table so there will be no problems when performing the forming.

Vacuum Table

The vacuum table needs only one hole if you are forming one object at a time (the buck needs to have small posts on the base or sit on a mesh to allow airflow). For multiple items, I place a pimpled rubber mat on the table so the airflow can pass under all objects.

Heating Unit

The heating unit is a pretty simple system made with a 1500-watt workshop heater, ¼″ particleboard, and aluminum foil (see plans).

The Frame

The frame holds the material that will be heated up. This frame is specifically designed for EVA foam. It has a 40-grit sanding belt glued to the inside.

Vacuum Cleaner

Make sure you have a strong vacuum cleaner. It doesn't have to be the best to work. I've been asked many times how many CFMs (vacuum cleaner airflow units) are needed. A simple answer would be between 80 and 120 CFMs, but airflow is not the most important thing to consider. The most important thing is how well the cleaner does under a load, whether it can keep a high-suction pressure going. One way to increase the suction power is to take the dust bag out of the vacuum cleaner. This helps a lot.

EVA Foam

Most EVA foam seems to work well for vacuum forming. I've used the cheap kind from building supply stores, the good foam from cosplay stores, and the super-strong medical foam. I've had success with 2–12mm low- and high-density EVA foam. At 16mm (½″), the foam was too thick to heat evenly enough to form over tall patterns and ended up ripping. I've concluded that unless the 16mm foam can be heated up slowly from both sides at the same time, you will be able to do only low-profile pulls when vacuum forming.

Thermoplastics

At my studio, I use ABS (Acrylonitrile Butadiene Styrene) and HIPS (High Impact Polystyrene) thermoplastics when I need a hard-shell item. The 18″ × 24″ unit has handled any thickness that is commonly used for vacuum forming.

Instructions

Amazon warrior armor using a homemade 24″ × 36″ vacu-former

/Tip/ *Plan on wasting some material as you learn the heating process. There is nothing like hands-on experience to help you learn not to burn.*

1 | Load the 4mm high-density EVA foam into the frame of the 18″ × 24″ vacuum former. Attach the front and side clamps, and double-check that they are secure.

STEP 1

2 | Make sure your heating device is clear of any foreign objects, and prepare to set the frame along with your material on top.

3 | Plug in the heating unit, and wait for it to get hot. It will take only a few minutes.

⚠ **SAFETY NOTE:** NEVER LEAVE ANY MATERIAL UNATTENDED OVER THE HEATING ELEMENT OF YOUR VACUUM FORMER, ESPECIALLY IF THE HEATING ELEMENT IS POSITIONED BELOW LIKE IN THIS DEMO. IF LEFT FOR TOO LONG, THE MATERIAL COULD MELT INTO THE HEATING ELEMENT AND POTENTIALLY CAUSE A FIRE OR OTHER DAMAGE.

STEP 2

4 | When it is hot, place the frame with the EVA foam onto the heating unit. Leave it there until you start to see the foam buckle a little bit.

5 | When the EVA foam becomes wavy, flip the frame over so the other side of the foam can start heating.

6 | When the foam starts to flatten out, flip the frame again, and continue to flip the frame about every minute until the foam is soft enough to be shaped.

/ Tip / *If you leave the heating on one side for too long the foam will burn. If this happens, make sure the unburned side of the foam is on top when you vacuum form it.*

STEPS 4–5

7 | When the foam is ready, turn on your vacuum, and take the frame off the heating unit. Line it up with the vacuum table guide, and press down as fast as you can until the frame makes contact with the table. As soon as the frame is flat against the vacuum table, the EVA foam will rapidly form around the pattern. Leave the vacuum cleaner on until the foam is cool enough to keep its form.

/ Note / *If you are too slow in doing this, the foam will be too cool to form properly and may even tear.*

/ Tips /

• *If on your first attempt the foam doesn't form properly, and if the foam hasn't ripped, you can reheat the EVA and try it again. When placing the frame back on the heating unit, the failed foam will heat up and flatten out again. You will have to keep flipping it until it's ready again.*

You may ruin a few pieces of foam before you get the knack of it.

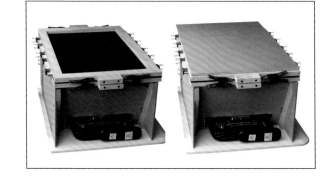

• *If the temperature is very cold where you are working, you will have a hard time keeping both sides of the foam hot enough for vacuum forming. One simple thing that helps is to place an 18″ × 24″ ½″ piece of plywood on top of your frame as you're heating. This keeps the top side of the foam from cooling too quickly as you flip the EVA.*

• *With ABS or HIPS thermoplastics, there can be no undercuts. If there are, you won't be able to get the pattern out of the molded plastic without cutting it, but with EVA foam, undercuts aren't as big a problem.*

8 | Unclamp the frame, and pull out the buck from the molded foam. You now have a great base to create a fun helmet, mask, or anything else.

9 | Draw the design and shapes you want for the eye holes and helmet shape.

10 | Cut out the eye holes and helmet boundaries.

11 | After cutting out the shape you want for your project, glue on the detail work. I normally would use contact cement, but for this example, I used quick spray glue (3M Super 77 spray adhesive). Then I placed my helmet back on the buck to get it ready for another round of vacuum forming.

Vacu-Form Layering

Vacuum forming can do more than just give you a base from which to work; it can give you a smooth, hard, or soft surface on top of your detail work.

You can vacuum form a soft shell on top of your helmet with 2mm high-density foam or make a hard shell using ABS or HIPS thermoplastic. With EVA foam, you'd use the same procedure that was previously done, but for thermoplastic, you'd need a different frame in which to secure the plastic.

Frame for Thermoplastic

The frame for thermoplastic is identical to the one used for foam, with one exception. Instead of the 40-grit sandpaper as shown in the plans, use a high-temperature neoprene rubber. Buy a sheet of it, and cut it into strips. Then, use contact cement to glue it to the wood frame. This provides a good surface to help hold the plastic in the frame when vacuum forming.

Second Layer of Vacu-Forming

1 | Place a plastic sheet into the frame, and clamp it down. I used 1mm HIPS thermoplastic.

Then on to the heater. Unlike foam, thermoplastic will start to sag when it's ready to form. With plastic this thin, flipping is not necessary.

2 | When you see a noticeable concave sag happening to the plastic, it is time to take the plunge. Turn on the vacuum table, line up the frame, and push down. As soon as the frame is flat against the vacuum table, the plastic sheet will rapidly form around the modified pattern. Leave the vacuum on until the material cools a little.

/Note/ *If the thermoplastic wasn't hot enough to form properly, you can place it back on the heating unit and try it again.*

⚠ **SAFETY NOTE:** NEVER LEAVE ANY MATERIAL UNATTENDED OVER THE HEATING ELEMENT OF YOUR VACUUM FORMER, ESPECIALLY IF THE HEATING ELEMENT IS POSITIONED BELOW LIKE IN THIS DEMO. IF LEFT FOR TOO LONG, THE MATERIAL COULD MELT INTO THE HEATING ELEMENT AND POTENTIALLY CAUSE A FIRE OR OTHER DAMAGE.

STEP 2

Now that you have the inner and outer shells, you can put them together and finish your project.

Special Thanks

To all the incredible individuals and brand names that have been part of our team along the way.

Makers

ALKALI ▶ Instructor

COREGEEK CREATIONS ▶ Judge, Instructor

CUTIEPIE SENSEI ▶ Judge

DAVID TOCK ▶ Owner

DIANA TOLIN ▶ Administrator

DOWNEN CREATIVE STUDIOS ▶ Judge, Instructor

THE EGG SISTERS ▶ Judge

EVIL TED SMITH ▶ Judge, Instructor

FROSTBITE COSPLAY ▶ Judge, Instructor

HDC FABRICATION ▶ Instructor

HOKU PROPS ▶ Owner, Administrator, Judge, Instructor

JACKIE CRAFT ▶ Judge

MULHOLLAND ART ▶ Instructor

PAISLEY AND GLUE ▶ Instructor

PANTERONA COSPLAY ▶ Judge

PAPA BEAR COSPLAY ▶ Judge

PLEXI COSPLAY ▶ Administrator, Instructor

POLYGON FORGE ▶ 2021 Best in Show, Judge

PROS AND CONS COSPLAY ▶ Judge

PUNISHED PROPS ACADEMY ▶ Judge

SAMEER TIKKA MASALA ▶ Instructor

SAMUI SAN ▶ 2020 Best in Show, Judge

SAYAKAT COSPLAY ▶ Instructor

SPARKLE STACHE ▶ Convention Programming

SPICY THAI DESIGN ▶ Judge

STELLA CHUU ▶ Judge

TIERZA89 ▶ 2021 Ultimate Cosplay Championship at Holiday Matsuri Best in Show

TIFFANY GORDON COSPLAY ▶ Administrator, Judge, Instructor

TOCK CUSTOM ▶ Owner, Host, Administrator, Instructor

TWIIN COSPLAY ▶ Convention Programming

VOLPIN PROPS ▶ Judge

YAYA HAN ▶ Judge

ZACH FISCHER ▶ Judge

Sponsors

ARDA WIGS

ARTOOL

BADGER AIRBRUSH

BERNINA

BROTHER INTERNATIONAL

C&T PUBLISHING

CORSAIR

COSPLAYSUPPLIES.COM

COS-TOOLS

CREATEX COLORS

DREMEL

DUFTWERKS

EPIC COSPLAY WIGS

FAMORÉ CUTLERY

HOLIDAY MATSURI

IWATA AIRBRUSH

KAMUI COSPLAY

KINPATSU COSPLAY

LUMECUBE

MAKE STICKERS

MANHATTAN WARDROBE SUPPLY

MEDEA

OVER 30 COSPLAY

PLAID CRAFTS/PLAIDFX

POLY-PROPS

PROP MONKEY STUDIOS

SHEPROP!

STAN WINSTON SCHOOL OF CHARACTER ARTS

SWEETYCON

TNT COSPLAY SUPPLY

TWITCH.TV

UNIQSO

UNITED SKULLS OF AMERICA

WACOM

WONDERFLEX WORLD

WORBLA

WULFGAR WEAPONS AND PROPS

How Ultimate Cosplay Began

On April 30, 2020, about two months into pandemic lockdown, Bryce of Frostbite Cosplay made a phone call to Tock Custom:

"Hey Tock. So … I've got a bunch of platinum silicone that's gonna go bad if I don't use it. What do you think of making a bunch of medals and trophies?"

"For what? Do you want to put on a virtual cosplay contest or something?"

"Yeah, I don't know, maybe?"

"Let me make some calls, and let's see if we can get some good judges together."

Forty minutes and a few phone calls later, they had confirmed a lineup of judges for their first competition, which had yet to be named. The Egg Sisters, Evil Ted, Frostbite Cosplay, Hoku Props, and Jackie Craft made up our judging panel, hosted by Tock Custom.

The next day they had a short meeting discussing details about how it could work. It started sounding very doable and extremely fun! The judges came up with a fantastic approach to running a smooth show, but the organizers got stuck on thinking of a good name for the contest. With mild frustration, Tock finally said, "All right, who cares. Let's just call it … the Ultimate … Online … Cosplay Championship," which everyone seemed happy with, and it stuck.

Later that night, they created a website and a submission form and started spreading the word. The competition would only be four weeks later, so they had to work quickly. The team really wanted to put on a fun community event that would let artists share their work while getting feedback from expert-level judges during a live show.

During the next few days, they received an enormous amount of enthusiasm from the community. They had cosplayers from around the world asking if they accepted international entries, sponsors wanting to contribute prizes, and costume makers sending personal videos to include in the program. By the time submissions closed, they had 297 entries from 34 countries, along with 19 sponsors. The team selected 50 finalists and had 13 total prizes. All the medals, trophies, and judges' choice awards were created from scratch by the contest panel. It truly was an incredible celebration for the cosplay community with support from around the world!

After the first show, cosplayers flooded the Ultimate Cosplay inbox with support and "When is the next one?!" messages. So Hoku Props, Tock Custom, and many others started planning ideas for what might be next. The Ultimate Cosplay brand has gone on to run a successful line of live and virtual competitions, podcasts, educational programming, workshops, panels, and convention presence. It's had participation from more than 40 countries, more than 30 sponsors, and hundreds of artists.

Since the beginning, Ultimate Cosplay has been a group of cosplayers creating events for people just like them because they love their community. It has been a privilege for the team to help celebrate this culture and help others grow with them.

Ultimate Cosplay

Website: ultimatecosplay.com

Facebook: facebook.com/UltimateCosplayChampionship

Instagram: @ultimatecosplaychampionship

Twitter: @cosplaychampion

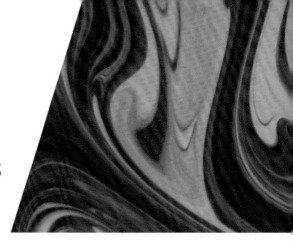

Author Biographies

Christopher Tock
TOCK CUSTOM

Christopher Tock is a self-taught fashion and costume designer from Milwaukee, Wisconsin. He is the owner of Tock Custom LLC, a men's clothing and accessory brand, and the cofounder of the Ultimate Cosplay Championship alongside Hoku Props and his brother David Tock. Starting in 2014, he created a cosplay for his first convention (Anime Milwaukee, 2015). It was such a successful venture that he didn't want to stop making new items, so he began learning new sewing projects such as dress shirts, men's jeans, and messenger bags. It wasn't long before Tock got into local art shows and craft fairs, started broadcasting his live workshop on Twitch.tv as a creative streamer, and began teaching new artists through videos.

Tock has since gone on to compete in several master class competitions, produce a very successful YouTube tutorial channel, work with industry sponsors, judge and host cosplay events, and collaborate with artists around the world. Tock is committed to supporting the creative culture through building community, producing cosplay programming, and teaching artists through any method available. His goal is to help create a safe, welcoming, and positive atmosphere for everyone who has the desire to create.

Character ▸ Lothar from *World of Warcraft*
Costume by Tock Custom

Tock Custom

Website: tockcustom.com

Facebook: facebook.com/tockcustom

Instagram: @tockcustom

Twitter: @tockcustom

Chad Van Wye
HOKU PROPS

Chad Hoku is the co-owner and founder of Hoku Props Inc., a small fabrication studio based in Southern California. Having grown up with a creative father, Chad was inspired to pursue a career in a creative field himself and started his journey by attending Gnomon— School of Visual Effects, Games & Animation in Hollywood, California. There he learned how to 3D model from some of the best in the industry before graduating from the University of California, Riverside, where he earned a bachelor's degree in business with a focus in arts management.

One of Chad's biggest passions is advocating for inclusivity and ensuring that everyone has access to knowledge. When he's not working, you can find him learning new skills or teaching others how to excel in their own creative passions. Chad has competed, judged, and consulted for cosplay competitions across the globe, and in 2020, he cofounded the Ultimate Cosplay Championship alongside Tock Custom. He hopes to continue making the cosplay community a place where everyone feels accepted and welcome.

A

Chad, with his wife Sammy and co-owner Jason of Hoku Props, were the grand prize winners of TwitchCon's first ever cosplay contest in 2016, with their "Larger than Life" Lionhardt cosplay from Blizzard's *Overwatch*. They have made out-of-this-world props and costumes together ever since.

Hoku Props

Website: hokuprops.com

Facebook: facebook.com/HokuProps/

Instagram: @hokuprops

Twitter: @hokuprops

B

A | Character ▶ Moon King, Original
Design by Chad Hatter (Chad Edward
Lee Evett)

Costume by Chad Hatter (Chad Edward
Lee Evett)

Photo by Brett Downen—Downen Photography

B | Character ▶ Lich King Bolvar Fordragon
from *World of Warcraft*

Original Costume Design by Zach
Fischer

Photo by Alexandra Lee Studios

Sammy Van Wye
HOKU PROPS

Sammy Hoku's love for cosplay started when she was at a young age; unbeknownst to her two mothers, giving their daughter a sewing machine for her thirteenth birthday would send her on an exciting and creative journey that she is still on to this day. This passion for cosplay and sewing eventually led Sammy to study fashion and costume design for her higher education, which helped her secure her first industry job at the Disneyland Resort, working in entertainment costuming. There she worked on various parades, special events, and her favorite show, *Aladdin: A Musical Spectacular*.

Sammy parted ways with Disney after almost five years but continued to fulfill her passion for creating costumes in her free time. She began cosplaying with Chad in 2015 and, through him, learned how to create props and armor out of a variety of materials. In 2016, Sammy, along with Chad and Jason of Hoku Props, competed in TwitchCon's very first cosplay contest; they took home grand prize with their "Larger than Life" Lionhardt cosplay from Blizzard's *Overwatch*.

Cosplay has played an integral role in Sammy's life, and without it, she never would have met her husband or developed some of her longest-lasting and strongest friendships. As the community continues to grow, she hopes to help others on their own journey into the cosplay world through the power of teaching and the written word.

A

Hoku Props

Website: hokuprops.com

Facebook: facebook.com/HokuProps/

Instagram: @hokuprops

Twitter: @hokuprops

A | Costume ▶ Sypha Belnades from *Castlevania* (Animated Series)

Photo by Alexandra Lee Studios

B | Character ▶ Alleria Windrunner from *World of Warcraft*

Original Costume Design by Zach Fischer

Photo by Alexandra Lee Studios